GPS *and* Geocaching *in* Education

Burt Lo

International Society for Technology in Education
EUGENE, OREGON • WASHINGTON, DC

GPS and Geocaching in Education
Burt Lo

Director of Book Publishing: *Courtney Burkholder*
Acquisitions Editor: *Jeff V. Bolkan*
Production Editors: *Tina Wells, Lynda Gansel*
Production Coordinator: *Rachel Williams*
Graphic Designer: *Signe Landin*
Developmental Editor: *Mike van Mantgem*
Copy Editor: *Kärstin Painter*
Proofreader: *Barbara J. Hewick*
Indexer: *Seth Maislin, Potomac Indexing*
Cover Design, Book Design, and Production: *Gwen Thomsen Rhoads*

SUSTAINABLE FORESTRY INITIATIVE
Certified Fiber Sourcing
Label applies to the text stock
www.sfiprogram.org

Library of Congress Cataloging-in-Publication Data
Lo, Burt.
 GPS and geocaching in education / Burt Lo.
  p. cm.
 Includes index.
 ISBN 978-1-56484-275-6 (pbk.)
 1. Geocaching (Game) 2. Global Positioning System. I. International Society for Technology in Education. II. Title.
 GV1202.G46L62 2010
 623.893–dc22

2010027062

First Edition
ISBN: 978-1-56484-275-6
Printed in the United States of America

Cover Photos: © iStockphoto.com/Susie Haines, © Burt Lo,
© iStockphoto.com/Shantell, © iStockphoto.com/Robert Dant
Inside Photos: Figure 1.2: © iStockphoto.com/BanksPhotos,
© iStockphoto.com/Lara Seregina, © iStockphoto.com/imagedepotro, © Apple,
© iStockphoto.com/Robert Dant, and © Navigadget; Figures 3.8–3.16: © Burt Lo

ISTE* is a registered trademark of the International Society for Technology in Education.

About ISTE

The International Society for Technology in Education (ISTE) is the trusted source for professional development, knowledge generation, advocacy, and leadership for innovation. ISTE is the premier membership association for educators and education leaders engaged in improving teaching and learning by advancing the effective use of technology in PK–12 and teacher education.

Home of the National Educational Technology Standards (NETS) and ISTE's annual conference and exposition (formerly known as NECC), ISTE represents more than 100,000 professionals worldwide. We support our members with information, networking opportunities, and guidance as they face the challenge of transforming education. To find out more about these and other ISTE initiatives, visit our website at www.iste.org.

As part of our mission, ISTE Book Publishing works with experienced educators to develop and produce practical resources for classroom teachers, teacher educators, and technology leaders. Every manuscript we select for publication is carefully peer-reviewed and professionally edited. We value your feedback on this book and other ISTE products. E-mail us at books@iste.org.

International Society for Technology in Education (ISTE)
Washington, DC, Office:
    1710 Rhode Island Ave. NW, Suite 900, Washington, DC 20036-3132
Eugene, Oregon, Office:
    180 West 8th Ave., Suite 300, Eugene, OR 97401-2916
Order Desk: 1.800.336.5191
Order Fax: 1.541.302.3778
Customer Service: orders@iste.org
Book Publishing: books@iste.org
Book Sales and Marketing: booksmarketing@iste.org
Web: www.iste.org

About the Author

Burt Lo is a technology professional development coordinator with the California Technology Assistance Project. He earned a master's of education degree in Information Technology and is a Google Certified Teacher. His instructional experience includes teaching middle school in California and teaching all ages in Taiwan. He has presented at state and national educational technology conferences to assist K–12 teachers with integrating video editing, podcasting, and Google Tools into their classrooms.

After becoming a geocaching fan and hobbyist, Burt began to use geocaching as an engaging teaching and learning activity in the classroom. This exploration has included investigating geocaching as part of the curriculum for a sixth grade outdoor education week in California and introducing geocaching to teachers and administrators during conference workshops.

Acknowledgments

This book would not have been possible without the support of many people. First and foremost, I would like to thank Sonny, Sandy, and Sean Portacio. Sonny and Sandy introduced me to geocaching during a session at the 2006 NECC in San Diego. In addition to getting me started with geocaching, they continue to expand my knowledge about geocaching through their weekly Podcacher podcast.

Secondly, I want to acknowledge Mike van Mantgem for providing assistance and guidance through the book writing process. It takes much more than ideas, time, and a word processor to write a book. Mike was an excellent guide through the entire process of organizing my ideas, making sure that content needed by new geocachers was included and selecting images that clarified the content.

Finally, I need to thank my family for their support for this project. Hopefully Vicky, Robert, Elizabeth, and Emma have enjoyed geocaching as much as I have enjoyed their company on our geocaching journeys.

Contents

CHAPTER 3

Caching Your World: A Quick Tour...................... 49

PART II

Geocaching in the Classroom and Beyond.......91

CHAPTER 4

Geocaching across the Curriculum 93

CHAPTER 5

Lesson Plans 105

ADVISORY

Students should be closely supervised when engaging in geocaching activities, whether on or off school premises. Neither the author nor ISTE shall be responsible for any injuries or damages that may occur as a result of geocaching activities.

An Introduction to Adventure

In 2006, while attending the National Educational Computing Conference (now known as the ISTE Conference and Exposition) in San Diego, I noticed that there were some hands-on sessions and presentations about geocaching. I had heard the term and had an understanding of the concept of geocaching, so I decided to spend part of the conference finding out more.

Fortunately, some geocaching zealots had also set up a geocaching course for conference attendees. This meant we could experience geocaching for ourselves. I found some time to explore downtown San Diego through the eyes of a geocacher and became hooked.

This book is my attempt to re-create that experience, and I would like nothing more than to introduce educators to the world of geocaching and to help them explore strategies for integrating geocaching into the classroom.

Geocache

A geocache is literally something hidden on Earth (from Greek *geo-*, earth, + French *cache*, pronounced cash, meaning to hide). Geocaching is a high-tech treasure hunting game. Geocachers equipped with coordinates and a GPS device find a cache and record their find online at www.geocaching.com.

That being said, it is difficult to fully convey the experience of geocaching in a book. Geocaching is a fun activity in its own right. It is also an exciting opportunity for student learning. So, in addition to reading this book, I recommend that educators go out and try geocaching before taking their students out for an adventure. I should mention that you don't have to try geocaching alone the first time out. Your local REI-style outdoors store may offer introductory GPS and geocaching workshops. Who knows? Maybe, like me, you'll be hooked the first time out—and immediately embrace the educational possibilities that geocaching offers.

Geocaching in the classroom provides teachers and students with a wide array of engaging educational activities. Simply speaking, geocachers acquire coordinates for a hidden treasure (cache), use a handheld Global Positioning System receiver (GPSr) to navigate to the coordinates, find the treasure, and log the find online. A recreational geocacher can find coordinates for nearby geocaches at the Official Global GPS Cache Hunt Site (www.geocaching.com). After putting the coordinates into a GPS receiver and lacing up some good walking shoes, the geocacher uses these coordinates to find geocaches hidden under mailboxes, in city parks, or along the sides of trails. Upon finding a geocache, the geocacher adds his or her name to the logbook in the geocache. This is physical proof of the find. To get "official" credit for finding the geocache, a player logs onto Geocaching.com and claims that find. However, in a classroom these simple steps have been used across different curricular areas for much more than simply finding treasure.

For example, geocaching can become an engaging activity that introduces students to their school campus. Instead of telling students the names of the principal and school nurse or the room number for the library, students can become modern-day explorers and locate this school information through a geocaching activity. Teachers can provide their students with a list of coordinates and a GPS device and ask students to identify the person or room located at each set of coordinates.

But geocaching can be used to do more than simply find predetermined locations. Geocaching can also be used as a thought-provoking review activity. Imagine that a class of students is studying the American Civil War. After presenting the causes of the war, teachers can verify student understanding in any number of ways. Teachers can have students simply fill out a worksheet, or they can provide students with a geocaching activity.

In such a geocaching activity, a teacher can create several geocaches that contain artifacts with information about the

United States at the time of the Civil War. The teacher might place a summary of the Emancipation Proclamation or a photo of Fort Sumter in a geocache. To get the students thinking about the causes of the Civil War, a list of government responsibilities could be included, and students could be asked to create two lists identifying which responsibilities belong to states and which belong to the federal government.

Additionally, the teacher could include a timeline of the events leading up to the Civil War and ask the geocaching teams to put the events in the correct chronological order. Artifacts such as these describe the differences between states' and the nation's rights, or the impact of the Fugitive Slave Law. These geocaches can then be placed in various locations around the school or in a nearby park, and be creatively labeled with names such as "The Emancipation Proclamation" or "Fort Sumter." Students would be provided with a GPSr and the coordinates of these geocache locations. In teams of union and confederate states, the students locate the geocaches. When a geocache is located, the teams interpret the information contained in the artifacts. Back in the classroom, the union and confederate teams discuss their findings and present what they feel are the reasons for going to war.

Finding geocaches is only half of geocaching. Creating and hiding geocaches is the other, and some would say more interesting, half—especially for educators. Of course, creating and hiding geocaches is what makes finding geocaches possible. More than that, it can also provide a variety of compelling learning activities. Almost any curricular subject can provide students with reasons for creating and hiding geocaches. For example, students might create and hide a geocache based upon a literature story or unit; the geocache could be named after a location in the book, and hidden in a manner that fits the story.

But geocaching isn't limited to the arts. In science education, for example, students are often asked to record their observations, which can be particularly challenging to students. However, when the areas of inquiry are created by a peer group, students can become very observant scientists. Perhaps a class is studying the weather, and the teacher would like students to record observations about temperature, humidity, cloud formation, and precipitation. Instead of asking students to retrieve this information from a newspaper or website, the teacher could challenge students to create and place geocaches that, in turn, their fellow students would locate in order to gather this information. This is an example of using the creation of a geocache as an effective learning activity.

In another example, a group of students could create a geocache that contained a disposable camera. When students find the geocache, they are asked to take a picture of the sky and identify the clouds by recording them in the geocache logbook. The answers proposed by the geocachers can be verified by the class after the photographs are developed.

As you can see, geocaching is not limited to a particular class or location, or even "official" caches listed on Geocaching.com. Students can also include a *Travel Bug* (TB) in a geocache. A travel bug is a dog-tagged item placed in a geocache that is meant to be picked up and moved along to other geocaches. Students can track online where the travel bug has moved and how far it has traveled from the original geocache.

As these examples demonstrate, geocaching can be both an enjoyable hobby and an engaging educational activity that can be used by both teachers and students. My hope is that this book furthers your knowledge of geocaching and provides you with ideas to get started in using it with your students.

Welcome to a world of adventure. Welcome to the world of geocaching.

About This Book

This book is designed to be as user-friendly as possible. Look for sidebars, tips, and hints to guide you. Additionally, this book is divided into two essential parts.

Part I

Think of this part as an introductory course on geocaching. If you've heard the word geocaching but not much more than that, Part I should be your starting point. This part opens with the basics of the Global Positioning System (GPS) and the activity of geocaching. Following this bit of groundwork, Part I continues with descriptions of the technology and terminology that educators (and students) need to know to become actual geocachers. Part I concludes with a section that is designed to help educators become geocaching savvy—an inservice of sorts that aims to help teachers introduce geocaching into the classroom.

Part II

For educators who have read Part I and/or have a handle on the basics of geocaching, Part II stands ready to assist you in implementing geocaching into your curricula. Look here for advice on real-world preparations, determining what skills students should acquire, and leading students on educational geocaching adventures. The Chapter 5 lesson plans are designed to be grade- and subject-specific, but I encourage you to be creative and adapt them to your particular teaching situation and style. The lesson plans support ISTE's National Educational Technology Standards for Students. The skills addressed in the professional development chapter, Chapter 6, support ISTE's National Educational Technology Standards for Teachers.

GPS and Geocaching

What do pirates, explorers, and geocachers have in common? A thirst for adventure. A restless desire to discover the wonders that lurk around the next bend, over the next hill, and beyond. And, of course, an insatiable craving for treasure.

Geocaching has been described as the world's largest treasure hunt. Unlike the explorers of yesteryear, who relied on magnetic compasses and parchment maps to find hidden treasures, today's geocachers rely on the out-of-this-world technology of the Global Positioning System (GPS). Instead of questing for pirate treasure, geocachers seek treasures hidden by other geocachers.

Students who encounter geocaching in the classroom are captivated by the creativity and real-world problem solving involved in creating and finding geocaches. Naturally, before you go on a geocaching adventure—and take along a class of students—you should have an understanding of what GPS is all about and what sort of treasures and pitfalls await.

Part I of this book is designed to help you:

- ▶ Understand the basics of GPS (and popular GPS devices)

- ▶ Get an overview of the geocaching landscape

- ▶ Become comfortable with geocaching lingo

These basics will help you:

- ▶ Decide what equipment and software you need

- ▶ Identify the many different types of geocaches

- ▶ Find and hide geocaches like a seasoned professional

- ▶ Resolve potential problems you might encounter

CHAPTER 1

Introducing GPS and Geocaching

Geocaching has been described as a worldwide treasure hunt or 21st-century orienteering. It is also accurate to say that geocaching is a classroom-friendly activity. To get involved, you and your class will be required to use a few essential tools and know a little bit about the technology behind the tools that make geocaching a reality. In this chapter you will:

- ▶ Learn the basics of GPS technology

- ▶ Get an overview of geocaching

- ▶ Go on a geocaching expedition with a class

What Is GPS?

As the name suggests, the Global Positioning System is a world-wide system of satellites that rotate around the world and beam location information back to Earth (Figure 1.1).

FIGURE 1.1. Artist's interpretation of GPS satellite.

Image courtesy of National Aeronautics and Space Administration (NASA).

The GPS system, developed and operated by the U.S. Department of Defense in the early 1970s, allows users with GPS receivers to determine their position on Earth. The U.S. military, under a directive ordered by President Ronald Reagan, declassified this system in 1983. Today, anyone can freely tap into the GPS system. To take advantage of the GPS system and become a geocacher, you need a GPS receiver.

GPS Receivers

GPS receivers (GPSrs) are now commonplace in all types of vehicles, watercraft, and aircraft (Figure 1.2). You might very well have a GPSr in your car that provides you with driving directions. For geocaching, a typical GPSr will triangulate a user's position to within about 3 meters (10 feet) of a specific location (latitude and longitude), anywhere in the world. The most popular type of GPSr in geocaching is a handheld device. These devices are commonly used by hikers and other outdoor enthusiasts.

FIGURE 1.2. GPS devices come in many different forms and sizes.

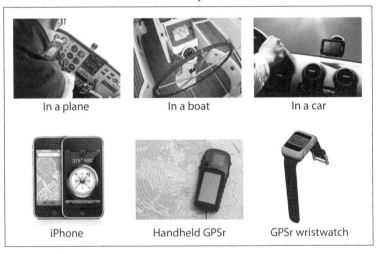

In a plane   In a boat   In a car

iPhone   Handheld GPSr   GPSr wristwatch

For most people, the GPS experience is as straightforward as driving their cars: They turn on their GPS receivers, enter their destination addresses, and follow the voice-guided turn-by-turn directions. But for the educator interested in geocaching, a GPS device is more than a fancy road map. It is a gateway to adventure with the geocaching community. It is an engaging tool for lesson planning with like-minded educators, and it invites students to use technology to meaningfully engage with the world outside the classroom walls.

Off the Map: Other Uses for GPS

▶ GPS can be used for more than navigation. For example, there are GPS receivers made specifically for use in timekeeping and scientific research. Because the clocks aboard GPS satellites keep the most accurate time in the world (universe?), astronomical observatories, telecommunications systems, and laboratories rely on this technology for precision timekeeping.

▶ Because GPS receivers allow users to precisely locate and mark a coordinate on Earth, the GPS system can be used for projects in the fields of civil engineering, agriculture, and earth sciences—ecology, geology, glaciology, volcanology, oceanography, atmospheric sciences, and so on.

▶ Many GPS receivers also include location-based games that can enrich physical education classes by providing virtual mazes or quests for students to complete. Because each student's activity is tracked and determined by the GPSr, an entire class of students can interact with their own activities while running around on the same playing field. For example, the Garmin GPSMap series of GPS receivers includes games such as:

1. *Virtual Maze.* A maze is displayed on the screen of the GPSr and the student is represented on screen. As the student moves around the playing field, the student marker moves in a similar fashion through the maze on

screen. The objective is to get through the maze and collect the on-screen flags as quickly as possible.

2. *Gekoids.* An asteroid field is displayed on the screen of the GPSr and the student is represented on screen. The student's objective is to avoid being hit by asteroids while shooting them. The student moves around the playing field to move their on-screen marker.

3. *Beast Hunt.* A partial maze is displayed on the screen of the GPSr and the student is represented on screen. The student's objective is to reveal the rest of the maze and find the dragon. The maze is revealed as the student moves around the playing field to move his or her on-screen marker. Upon finding the dragon, the student engages in battle with the dragon to end the hunt.

Of course, the GPS system and GPS receivers are merely the means to an end. To focus our attentions on the GPS technology is a bit like going on a hike and obsessing about the map while ignoring the scenery. So, what sort of scenery does a GPSr allow us to see? Let's dive deeper into the world of geocaching.

What Is Geocaching?

Cache (pronounced *cash*) comes from the French word *cacher*, which means "to hide." A geocache, then, is a hiding place or something stored in a cache. Geocaching is an activity in which participants place and find hidden items (caches) located at specific locations (waypoints) with the assistance of a GPS device and an online database of these waypoints, Geocaching.com. This is the simple concept that drives geocaching.

Waypoints, Placemarks, and POIs

The term *waypoint* is as old as geocaching itself. Today, geocachers use the term *placemark*, a Google Maps term, as a synonym for *waypoint*. Additionally, many new GPS devices use the term *Point of Interest* (POI) to stand in for *waypoint*.

Geocaches take many shapes, sizes, and forms—from smaller than a matchbox, to a 55-gallon drum, to a heroic monument, or a specific spot on Earth. These caches, and many more, are detailed in Chapter 2.

At this point you might have a lot of questions: How are geocaches placed? Who places them? How do I find out about the existence of a geocache? How do I locate a geocache (once I know it exists)? What sort of GPSr do I need to go geocaching? Are any geocaches located near me? What do I do when I find one?

Never fear. Answers to these questions and more are just a few pages away.

While geocaching lesson plans reside in Part II of this book (specific activities with specific outcomes), on a more general level, it's worth mentioning that geocaching provides students with a way to focus and shape not only an outdoor excursion but their interactions with the larger community of real-world adventurers.

In my experience, students love geocaching for a variety of reasons—the very real possibility of finding hidden treasure is chief among them. (Who doesn't love the idea that treasure is hidden everywhere around us, right under our very noses, just waiting to be found?) But students also love geocaching because it is a self-directed adventure with clear rules, parameters, and outcomes. They love to discover, create, and hide their own geocaches. They like to participate in this community of treasure seekers. And they like the technology itself—it's fun and easy to use. Geocaching is a world where technology meets adventure. All you have to do is find it. That's where the fun begins.

A Week of Geocaching

One of the greatest joys of spending a week at outdoor education with my sixth grade class is being outside the four walls of our classroom. Our county office of education provides an outdoor school, complete with cabins, trails, and even certified naturalists for use by schools during the academic year. The naturalists have prepared lessons that introduce the significance of earth forms located in the area, demonstrate how compost is created, or explore the pH of local streams. Teachers bring their classes to this outdoor setting to study the environment and science in a hands-on setting. The program provides an opportunity to engage in learning activities, including geocaching, that take advantage of the unique environment. Although my school introduces students to geocaching during outdoor education, my students enjoy variations of these activities back at school, and at home.

The first geocaching activity involves getting the students familiar with both the layout of the outdoor education site and how to use GPS receivers. I work with one of the naturalists on staff to put the coordinates of several important locations of the outdoor education site into the GPS receivers. Then the students, the naturalist, and I set out on our first hike. On the way to the first coordinates, I demonstrate to the students how to recall coordinates on the GPSr and how to use the pointer to locate landmarks along the trail.

After the naturalist explains the importance of the location, the students are asked to guide the group to the next set of coordinates. After each student has had a chance to use the GPS receivers, the naturalist leads the class to new locations, whose coordinates have not been stored in the GPS receivers. At these locations, students are shown how to mark coordinates in the GPS receivers.

Upon returning to the main lodge, students exchange GPS receivers with another class of students and try to find each other's coordinates. After successfully locating the coordinates, the classes meet again to discuss the significance of these marked locations. This is a fun way to introduce students to the outdoor "classroom" and to GPS receivers.

After students have been introduced to the outdoor education classroom, the focus turns to content. Because our outdoor education site has been home to a Native American tribe and has many real-life science exhibits, there are many subjects that can be used as content for geocaches. The naturalists help create and hide several geocaches that contain artifacts that students need to study. Some geocaches contain clues to the lifestyles of the Native

Americans who once lived in the area. Other geocaches contain scientific experiments for students to observe or measure about its location.

The class is divided into groups, and each group is provided with a GPSr, a list of coordinates and instructions, and a voice recorder. Each group member is provided with a job: using the GPSr to guide the group to the geocache; recording the information required at the geocache; or gathering information needed to guide the group to the next geocache. Upon finding a geocache, the group works together to follow the geocache instructions and script a response that records the geocache find.

For example, a group might find a geocache located at the side of a creek. Inside the geocache, students find a thermometer and a pH indicator. The students are asked to record the temperature and pH of the creek, determine the water's acidity, and observe the organisms in the water. After completing the tasks for the geocache, group members switch jobs and move to the next geocache. At the next geocache, the group might find themselves at a building that was once used by the Me-Wuk tribe. Inside the geocache, there is a magnifying glass, a measuring tape, paper, and color pencils. The group is asked to record observations about the structure, sketch the tribe using the structure, and record the answer about how they think the structure was used by the tribe. After completing the list of geocaches, the groups discuss their answers with each other and the naturalist to check their observations and conclusions.

As the week at outdoor education winds down, the naturalists and I look for ways to review the content with students. A popular method for this review includes content-related puzzles as part of geocaching activities. By this point, the students have become adept at both entering coordinates into the GPS receivers and using the GPS receivers to recall coordinates and navigate to locations. After selecting contents, tasks, and locations for geocaches, the naturalists and I devise puzzles (review activities) that students must solve to complete the geocaches' coordinates.

For example, students may be provided with the following WGS 84 coordinates:

$$N\ 38°\ 01.ABC\ W\ 120°\ 20.DEF$$

This example of the WGS 84 coordinates use minutes to describe the points between degrees. Thus, *N 38° 01.ABC W 120° 20.DEF* is read as: "North 38 degrees, 1-point-ABC minutes; West 120 degrees, 20-point-DEF minutes."

Read this way, it's clear that *ABC* and *DEF* are placeholders for missing coordinates.

The goal of this exercise is for students to fill in the missing coordinates (*ABC* and *DEF*), and then use the completed coordinates to locate another geocache. Students find the missing coordinates by completing a sequence of review activities.

The review begins when, in groups, students navigate to the first known geocache in the sequence (complete coordinates are provided, or students can complete an activity, quiz, or puzzle to get those coordinates).

Student teams find the geocache and complete the activity that has been placed there. For example, students may be asked to summarize the significance of the geocache location and record an important tip or factoid that will be shared with the next group of students who visit the outdoor education classroom. In that geocache, the coordinates for the next geocache are also provided (or students can complete an activity, quiz, or puzzle to get those coordinates). Students then navigate to the next geocache and continue the review. The final geocache contains an activity that, when completed, reveals the missing coordinates *ABC* and *DEF*. Students then hunt for the "first" geocache to complete the review. Students not only enjoy the challenge but they love the sense of completion when the "first" cache is found.

Know the Code

GPS coordinates can be presented in at least four different formats: WGS 84, NAD27, NAD83, and UTM. The most current format for representing GPS coordinates is known as WGS 84 (World Geodetic System of 1984). This format represents coordinates using Hemisphere (HDD) and Minutes in decimal format (MM.MMM).

Other common formats that enjoyed greater popularity prior to WGS 84 are NAD27 (North American Datum 1927) and NAD83 (North American Datum 1983). NAD27 based coordinates in relation to the latitude and longitude of an initial point (Meades Ranch in Kansas). NAD83 based coordinates on a more advanced image of the global sphere and did not rely upon the coordinates of an initial point. A fourth format for representing GPS Coordinates is UTM (Universal Transverse Mercator). This format divides the globe into 60 zones.

This is an educational variant of a *multi-cache* (also known as an *offset cache*). How straightforward or complicated the puzzles found in each cache are is limited only by your imagination, the temperament of your students, and the material you want to be reviewed. Site-specific quizzes, cumulative logic puzzles, crosswords, anagrams—all are fair game.

CHAPTER 2

Getting Started: Geocaching Basics for Educators

L ike any famous explorer, before embarking on a geocaching expedition you must first prepare for adventure. It goes without saying that you should be thoroughly familiar with the world of geocaching before you hit the trail or lead a group of students into the wild (or at least out onto the school grounds). Consider this chapter as your first big step into that world. Read on to:

- ► Get familiar with handheld GPS receivers

- ► Learn how to create a free account at Geocaching.com

- ► Discover the types of caches near you

Fortunately, learning the geocaching basics is not too difficult—and it's also a lot of fun.

Tools of the Trade: Popular GPS Receivers

A Global Positioning System receiver (GPSr) harnesses information from the Global Positioning System. The information taken from the GPS system will help you find geocaches. A GPSr and a magnetic compass are the only pieces of equipment you must purchase to participate in geocaching.

While you may already have a GPSr for your car (or boat or plane) that provides you with turn-by-turn directions, geocaching requires a GPSr in which you are able to input specific latitude and longitude coordinates. The most popular handheld GPSr devices are manufactured by Garmin and Magellan and are well-suited for geocaching. Moreover, these devices are suitable for classroom use and are relatively inexpensive—as of this writing, you can find them new for approximately $100 each.

FIGURE 2.1. Garmin's eTrex Legend and Magellan's Triton 200 are two GPS receivers suitable for classroom geocaching.

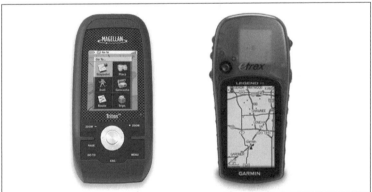

If I Had to Choose ... Magellan vs. Garmin

Both of these manufacturers offer a wide variety of GPSr receivers suitable for geocaching. Of course, other companies, notably Bushnell and DeLorme, make handheld GPS receivers. But Magellan and Garmin are the Marco and Polo of the industry.

Both Magellan and Garmin offer models that range from inexpensive, stripped-down basic GPS units to high-end, niche-specific units. Magellan offers its devices through a few basic categories (a single line of handheld devices and two lines specifically designed for driving). Garmin offers six distinct categories, each with its own extensive line of products.

It's worth noting that Garmin offers a "no mapping" line of handhelds—these devices save and display waypoints but do not feature maps. These "no mapping" devices are not necessarily less expensive than those that feature mapping. Mapping is an important feature for GPS receivers intended to be used for geocaching: maps allow you to see what sort of terrain and obstacles are ahead of you, such as hills, streams, roads, and airports—places you might not be able to easily walk through. Thus, for geocaching I recommend handheld GPS receivers that feature mapping. My choice for a classroom GPSr is Garmin's eTrex Legend H because of its cost and included USB cable for downloading coordinates. I also use a Garmin GPSMap 60 and iPhone for personal geocaching. Ultimately, the choice is yours.

Like many modern electronic devices, handheld GPS receivers feature an overload of options, but there are a few essentials that beginners—students and teachers alike—need to know. If you've never held a GPSr, you can use the following information to narrow your choices when selecting a GPSr for geocaching. If you're a GPSr pro, the following is a reminder of the basic GPSr features that your students should understand prior to a geocaching adventure.

Durability

Rain, drops, spills, and a hundred eager hands. If a group of students can do harm to a handheld electronic device— unintentionally or otherwise—they will. Someday. So the question isn't if your class set of GPS receivers will get dropped, lobbed, rained-on, or mistreated, it's a question of how well the devices can handle years of rough treatment. You should short-list models that feature rubber grips with as few buttons and breakable parts as possible and avoid devices with hinged flaps and exterior antennas.

Suitability

As for geocaching with dashboard-mountable GPS receivers designed for driving ... don't even think about using them with your class. They are not suitable.

Battery Life

No matter where you lead your students on a geocaching hunt, be it in the backwoods or on the school playground, the battery life of your GPSr matters—a lot. Each device has a factory-listed battery rating in terms of hours or minutes, regardless if the device relies on disposable batteries or features a built-in rechargeable battery. (Bottom line: the more hours the better.) Using disposable batteries means waste; using rechargeable batteries means cord management and good planning. Devices with color displays drain battery power much more quickly than units with black-and-white displays. You know yourself and your students better than anyone else. Choose wisely.

Ease of Use

Applicable to all popular electronic devices, a phenomenon called "feature creep" is a real issue. Ever notice that software updates contain more features and not less? Ever notice how electronic devices never get *less* complicated from one year to the next? This is feature creep. In this regard, GPS receivers have suffered the same fate as other electronic gadgets. Truth be told, many GPS receivers have complicated whizbang features that you and your students will *never* use for geocaching. Narrow your choices to handheld GPS receivers that have big, easy-to-use buttons and a crisp, clear display that is bright enough to see even in the midday sun. Choose a GPSr that can be used with one hand. Keep it simple.

Mapping

As mentioned earlier in this chapter in the "If I Had to Choose … Magellan vs. Garmin" box, I recommend that your GPS receiver(s) feature mapping. It is important to see terrain and obstacles.

Budget

Educators don't need me to say anything about budgets. Suffice it to say that the more basic the GPS receivers you use, the less expensive they should be. Look for bargains. Hunt on eBay.

Teach@15 Award: A Tale of Hidden Treasure

In 2005, a teacher at my school won a Best Buy Teach Grant. This yearly award, sponsored by the technology retailer Best Buy, was designed to help schools meet their technology needs. That teacher used the award to purchase 10 GPSrs—the beginnings of a full classroom set. It was these devices that introduced me to the world of geocaching. The Teach Award has been replaced by the Teach@15 Award (http://at15.com/contests_scholarships/teach_rules).

However, *I do not recommend that you mix-and-match GPS devices* in order to build a classroom set—managing too many different devices will create innumerable and unnecessary distractions for you and your students.

PC Interface

Most GPS receivers have the capability to connect directly with a personal computer (PC). Make certain that yours *has* the ability to interface with a PC, either via data cable, data port, or wireless. With this sort of connectivity, a GPSr can download hundreds of GPS waypoints in moments. Without this feature, you or your students must enter the coordinates of each prospective geocache into the devices by hand, or copy the coordinates down with pen and paper. While this handwork is an important skill to learn, after students have mastered this operation, it is more efficient to download the geocache coordinates into the receivers directly and spend valuable learning time hunting for geocaches.

Software

Quality handheld GPS receivers, like any computer peripheral, are designed to interface with Internet-connected computers that run on popular operating systems (Windows, Mac OS). Through this interface, manufacturers like Garmin and Magellan are able to continually update the software for their devices—operating systems, maps, and the like. Before you purchase a classroom set of GPS receivers, make certain the model you choose will interface with the type of computer that your school or district supplies and supports.

The Compass: A Low-Tech Solution to a High-Tech Problem

Without a doubt, GPS is the best system ever devised for getting around our world. But it is not perfect, at least in terms of geocaching. Enter the magnetic compass.

Let me start by saying that a GPSr is not an electronic compass. A GPSr works by triangulating its position relative to satellites in space and known locations on Earth. The compass that's displayed on a GPSr is, in actuality, an indicator. This indicator works extremely well under a few key conditions, namely that you have a good satellite connection and you keep moving. But once you find yourself under a canopy of trees (thus blocking the line-of-sight to an open sky) and getting close to a cache (meaning that you're walking slower), the compass "needle" on your GPSr will jump about. Worse still, the more cover above you and the slower you go, the more unreliable your GPSr compass will be. What to do?

Continued

Why, go low-tech, of course! Using a compass allows you to realign a cache when your GPSr indicator starts spinning, which happens when you stop near a cache (especially if a lot of cover is overhead). Consult a compass as you find yourself naturally slowing your pace when approaching a cache. With a compass, you can go as slowly as you want and forage under as many bushes as you deem reasonable without getting lost. Geocachers who work in small groups can use a compass in tandem with a GPSr to triangulate their approach to a cache.

Before you go geocaching get a reliable magnetic compass. Your compass doesn't need to be the very best quality, but it should not be the cheapest either. Read reviews; shop around.

Finally, as any experienced backcountry hiker will tell you, a quality magnetic compass and a map are essential equipment prior to venturing into the great unknown. As great as GPS receivers are, they require batteries. This is a problem. Miles from nowhere with the sun going down, it is folly to rely solely on a battery-powered GPSr to navigate home.

Geocaching with Smartphones and iPod Touch

Combining the power of a personal computer and the convenience of a handheld device, smartphones (such as the iPhone or Android phones) and mobile handheld devices (such as the iPod Touch) may be the perfect geocaching devices. An added bonus is that some of your students may already have one of these devices, meaning your classroom may already have some GPS receivers.

Many smartphones pull double duty as an Internet-ready device and GPSr. Provided cell phone coverage is available, smartphone users can access Geocaching.com on the fly to search, browse, research, and log caches. Because the latest generation of smartphones have good built-in GPS receivers, these devices perform the essential functions of a handheld GPSr even when cell coverage isn't available. Mobile devices such as the iPod Touch can also function as a GPSr (see the sidebar, Geocaching with the iPod Touch, on page 32). The iPod Touch and iPad, like the iPhone, need Internet access to in order to utilize Geocaching.com. There is potential for using the iPad for geocaching, but its size keeps it from being a very practical GPS device. Android devices such as the Dell Streak also have potential for geocachers.

Cell Phones in the Classroom?

Cell phones and students have an uneasy relationship in the classroom. In fact, many school districts ban or limit the use of personal electronic devices during school hours.

Consult your school policies and administration, and check in with parents, before asking your students to use personal cell phones for school work. Parental approval and charges to individual cell phone plans are issues that need to be taken seriously.

In terms of geocaching, the downside of these devices lies in the expense, the durability of the devices themselves, and battery life. If you're geocaching on school grounds with your regular class, these issues aren't likely a cause for concern. But if you're geocaching in the backwoods with a troop of scouts, in the rain, and miles from nowhere, the durability and longevity of your GPSr is mission-critical. For this reason, smartphone-enabled geocachers who venture into the backwoods often take along a stand-alone GPSr for backup.

Regardless, smartphones and geocaching are superbly compatible—loading, tracking, and logging caches is quick, easy, and incredibly convenient. If a smartphone or iPod Touch will be your primary geocaching tool, I recommend that you purchase a geocaching application. Geocaching-specific apps are continuously updated, and new applications are being created all the time. To see the latest for smartphone apps, tap your way to Groundspeak's Geocaching

Geocaching with the iPod Touch

The iPod Touch is designed for fun and games. It can even stand in for a GPSr, provided that a WiFi signal is within reach. That's great—except that WiFi signals are typically local Internet access points. A WiFi signal often doesn't appear in the backwoods.

What's needed, of course, is an iPod Touch with GPS functionality. It just so happens that an easy-to-use hardware add-on does just that. The "GPS Navigation & Battery Cradle for iPod Touch" from Dual Electronics is a slim device that slips onto the iPod Touch and transforms it into an iPhone-like GPSr. The cost is under $200.

iPhone Apps (www.geocaching.com/iphone) and Android Apps (www.geocaching.com/android).

For those new to geocaching, Groundspeak also has a free iPhone application called Geocaching Intro that finds the three closest geocaches to your location. Not only does this application guide you to the nearest geocaches, it also walks you through the steps of geocaching as you go.

But I Don't Have an iPhone!

No worries. Geocache Navigator (www.geocachenavigator.com) is a mobile application designed for non-iPhone users. Developed by Trimble, in partnership with Groundspeak, this application is compatible with a huge variety of carriers and GPS-enabled cell phones and smartphones. Taking advantage of a smartphone's GPS capabilities and wireless data networking abilities, Geocache Navigator transforms a smartphone into a high-quality GPSr.

Geocache Navigator is a killer application. The designers of this software spent a lot of time troubling through the details, and it shows. The interface is easy and intuitive, even for the novice, thus allowing users to concentrate on the hunt without getting lost in menus and screens. The same can be said for function-ality: The map features, compass, and interface with the database of caches on Geocaching.com all work very well. Moreover, the Geocache Navigator website is well designed, easy to use, and informative.

As great as the Geocache Navigator application is, it has a few catches. Like the comparable iPhone application, Geocache

Navigator requires solid cell coverage to work. Unlike the iPhone application, it is free to download, but it is in truth a pay-as-you-go monthly service. This service typically runs approximately $6 per month, though prices and service schemes vary by carrier. In the short term, this is a less expensive option than purchasing a new handheld GPSr (or an iPhone), but usage means data transfer, which may or may not be an issue, depending on your service plan. And, like the iPhone, depending on the type of geocaching you do and the type of smartphone you use, durability and battery life may be an issue.

Other GPSr Manufacturers

Of course, the world of GPS receivers is covered by more than the manufacturers and models mentioned previously. A quick web search will reveal a plethora of handheld devices suitable for geocaching. Other notable manufactures include:

► Bushnell: www.bushnell.com/products/gps

► DeLorme: www.delorme.com

The World Wide Web: Finding Caches Near You

Now that you have a handle on handheld GPS devices, you're ready to go geocaching. But where are the treasures hidden? Luckily, a few key websites provide you with complete access to the world of geocaching. Each website mentioned here helps users to experience a slightly different type of geocaching.

Geocaching.com

This website, run by Groundspeak (www.groundspeak.com), hosts the database of official geocaches. This is by far the most important online location for geocachers. Through this site, anyone in the world can place and find geocaches. It's as simple as that. Easy and fun to use, informative, and dynamic—Geocaching.com is essentially a giant database that allows users to post information about the physical caches they hide, provide the waypoints of those caches (a.k.a. coordinates), plus clues, hints, riddles, and other relevant information. Geocache hunters then sort through these postings to find caches close to them—via a combination of filters that include zip code, cache type, size, and difficulty—with the aid of GPS coordinates, icons on an embedded Google map, and other hints.

Geocaching without the Web

This section outlines the cache-finding process on Geocaching.com and other sites simply because it is something that every geocacher must know. However, to take a group of students on a geocaching expedition you don't necessarily need to rely on geocaches found on sites like Geocaching.com. In fact, sometimes you shouldn't. Reasons for this are outlined elsewhere:

► Geocaching in Education: Finding Caches without Geocaching.com (page 64)

► Listing Guidelines: Geocaching.com (page 89)

Tips and Forums

Geocaching.com hosts a robust forum. Not only can you find answers to basic (and not so basic) questions, you will find a vigorous online community discussing every imaginable aspect of geocaching. Interestingly enough, educators make up a large part of the geocaching community. This segment of the geocaching community is very active in the forums and shares opinions on which GPS receivers to use in the classroom, where to find GPS receivers for the best prices, and geocaching lesson ideas. Jump in, learn, and share!

Geocachers often research caches prior to going on field trips, vacations, or business trips. After hunters go into the real world and find a cache, they return to the website to get credit for finding it and post feedback regarding their hunt, the status of the cache itself, photos, and other information.

The tone of the website is lighthearted and convivial—it is a welcoming place for geocachers of all ages and skill levels. Likewise, the site provides an abundance of geocaching information: community guidelines, tutorials, helpful software and user-generated tools, forums; links to educational resources, hardware manufacturers, newsgroups/podcasts/webzines; and related activities such as orienteering, money tracking, letterboxing, and team building.

To use the services provided on Geocaching.com, you are required to create an account. Geocaching.com offers two levels of membership, free and premium. Until you become an avid geocacher, the free membership offers all the tools you need to find, hide, and enjoy geocaches with your students.

To create a free account at Geocaching.com, simply visit the website and click on the link Create a Membership! at the top of the page. On the subsequent signup page, click the Get a Basic Membership button and follow the instructions.

Geocaching.com currently offers one type of premium membership with two different pricing tiers ($30 per year, or $10 for three months). If the geocaching bug bites you hard, consider a premium membership that provides you with features that include: instant notifications about newly published caches (if you're among the first to know about a new cache, you have a chance to be the first to find it); custom sorts and searches based on cache size, location, and other attributes; an organizing tool that allows you to create favorites lists; and more.

Perhaps the most important feature of the premium account is that it allows users to create Pocket Queries (PQs)—files that can contain up to 500 geocache coordinates. These files are automatically generated according to a user's preset criteria and can be instantly uploaded directly to your GPSr or smartphone. Pocket Queries can be filtered by any number of parameters, including number of caches, cache type, container size, and location. For the latest about Pocket Queries, please visit the My Pocket Queries section of the Geocaching website (http://geocaching.com/pocket).

Avid geocachers have been known to find the newest caches during their lunch hour. Don't be surprised if, someday, this is you.

Waymarking.com

This site, also run by Groundspeak (www.groundspeak.com), allows users to create virtual caches. Unlike a more traditional geocache, which is a physical object of some kind, a virtual cache is a location—an interesting landmark, a vista point—that's notable enough to cache. These virtual caches provide a way to geocache in areas where traditional geocaching is not permitted. (For instance, placing geocaches in U.S. National Parks is not an approved practice.) Waymarking.com provides participants with an opportunity to find specific locations and take pictures or answer location-specific questions to verify their find.

Other similar cache types found on the Waymarking.com website include webcam and locationless caches. For webcam caches, geocachers find a webcam that's operated by a tourist attraction, for example, and have someone save their picture as they appear on the webcam (easier said than done). Locationless caches are a sort of reverse cache; instead of locating a container by using coordinates, geocachers locate a specific object and provide its coordinates. The coordinates are logged in as the treasure.

Waymarking.com offers two levels of membership, free and premium. To create an account, locate the membership sign-in box and click on the link Create a New Membership or Create a Free Membership. Users who create an account at Geocaching.com can use that account information to log in to Waymarking.com.

EarthCache.org

Operated by the Geological Society of America (GSA), the EarthCache website (www.earthcache.org) allows users to find and develop geocaches specifically for the geosciences—the study of our Earth. Official EarthCaches are hosted on Geocaching. com. Users need a Geocaching.com account to locate or create an EarthCache.

An EarthCache is a virtual geocache with an expressly educational twist. The idea is for players to gain insight into the geological processes that shaped a given site, how scientists study Earth, how we can manage our precious resources, and other issues. The treasures in these geocaches are not physical objects but educational lessons.

To create an EarthCache, users must not only designate a site but also create an earth science lesson that treasure seekers must complete. Each EarthCache is approved by GSA before it is posted on Geocaching.com. Complete guidelines for finding and creating EarthCaches are found at the EarthCache website. Look for the EarthCache Sites for Teachers page (www.geosociety.org/ Earthcache_Lessons).

EarthCaches are not limited to the United States. A recent Best 10 List at EarthCache included EarthCaches from Canada, Portugal, Sweden, Australia, and the U.S.

Confluence.org

The Degree Confluence Project is yet another way that geocaching brings geography to life for students. Users of this site post pictures of themselves taken where lines of latitude and longitude intersect. Students may see the lines on maps and globes, but this project and a GPSr allow them to actually visit the places where those lines "exist."

Other Geocaching-Related Websites

By no means is the world of geocaching limited to the previously mentioned websites. In the interest of filling out this picture, I should mention a few other geocaching-related sites. These sites offer educators interesting geocaching options and enhancements.

Wherigo.com. Operated by Groundspeak, Wherigo (pronounced *Where I go*) is actually a gaming platform that allows users to create GPS-enabled game files, called cartridges. Players download these files but they don't play the game on a computer; they play in the real world! For more details about this type of cache, see the section "Wherigo: The Ultimate Virtual Multi-Cache" in Chapter 3. Additionally, see the role-playing game (RPG) lesson plan "Real World RPG" in Chapter 5 for specific ideas for bringing Wherigo into the classroom.

Bookcrossing.com. This is the largest lending library in the world, and many people probably don't know it exists. Bookcrossing enthusiasts "register and release" their books. They tag a book with a unique number and leave it some-where in the big, wide world. The idea is that another person will pick it up and read it, post their find on the site, and then "lend it" again. You may not travel the world, but your favorite characters just might.

Letterboxing North America (www.letterboxing.org). A low-tech version of geocaching, letterboxing is a game in which players both hide and find waterproof boxes that typically contain a logbook, a unique rubber stamp, and an inkpad. Clues to finding letterboxes are posted online or are passed by word of mouth. Players who find a letterbox use the rubber stamp to mark their personal logbook, and mark the logbook in the letterbox with their own personal stamp.

Geocaches: Size, Type, and Difficulty

Digital compass (a.k.a. GPSr) in one hand, virtual treasure maps in the other (thanks to the many geocaching websites), and you're finally ready to embark upon a geocaching expedition. But what sorts of treasures are hidden in the world around you? Indeed, what do geocaches look like? And how difficult are they to find?

A cache can take many shapes and be many things. Typically, a cache is some sort of container that holds the treasure that hunters seek. A cache is categorized in three essential ways: size, type, and difficulty.

Know the Lingo

Geocaching, like any other activity, has its own secret language. It's part of the fun. But it's no fun at all when you don't know the lingo. Consult Appendix B, Glossary of GPS and Geocaching Terminology, at the back of this book, and you'll be at Ground Zero (GZ) in no time.

Size

An official geocache is typically organized into one of four sizes: micro, small, regular, and large. The person who places the cache designates a cache's size based on the following guidelines.

Micro

A microcache can be any container that is large enough to hold a scrap of paper (the log sheet) and maybe a golf pencil. Think of something the size of a 35mm film canister or a breath mints container—or smaller.

FIGURE 2.2. An example of a micro-sized cache.

Photo courtesy of Flickr user Cachemania.

Small

The typical small cache is about the size of a plastic sandwich container. This container is large enough to hold the basics (a golf pencil and a log sheet) along with a few prizes.

FIGURE 2.3. An example of a small-sized cache.

Photo courtesy of Flickr user Cachemania.

Regular

Although a container of this size can hold up to five gallons of treasure, this size of cache is usually approximately the size of a shoebox. Military surplus ammo boxes are standard-issue containers for this size.

FIGURE 2.4. An example of a regular-sized cache.

Photo courtesy of Flickr user Cachemania.

Large

Large caches hold more than five gallons of treasure. Large cache containers can be quite big—as large as a 55-gallon drum, or larger.

FIGURE 2.5. An example of a large-sized cache.

Photo courtesy of Flickr user Piglicker.

Type

In addition to size, caches are also categorized by type. While a geocache can be anything, the types applicable to education share a few common features.

Traditional/Typical

At its most basic level, a traditional geocache consists of a water-proof container, a piece of paper (a log sheet or logbook), and a writing implement (a golf pencil). For educational purposes, a traditional cache can contain items for learning activities that are relevant to that cache and its location.

Multi-Cache/Offset Cache

As the name implies, this is a set of related caches. Multi-caches typically begin with one cache that contains hints for finding a second cache; the second cache contains hints for finding a third cache, and so on. The final cache in the chain is considered to be the actual cache.

Puzzle Cache

This type of geocache requires players to solve some sort of puzzle or puzzles to find the cache itself. These puzzles can range from getting waypoint coordinates by solving a Sudoku to puzzles requiring a special code ring to find the solution.

Letterbox Hybrid

Using clues, and sometimes GPS coordinates, letterboxing is a lower-tech version of geocaching. See Letterboxing North America in the previous section of this chapter.

EarthCache

This type of geocache is not a physical object but an educational lesson about the features of Earth.

Virtual Cache/Webcam Cache

These geocaches are not physical objects per se, but locations on Earth. To get credit for finding these caches, players need to answer questions about the cache location or have their picture taken at the cache site.

Difficulty

Some geocaches are very easy to find, others are nearly impossible. After players hide a cache, they typically go to Geocaching. com and list their stash. Besides detailing the cache's features (size, type), they also rate how difficult it will be for someone else to find the cache. Difficulty is rated in two categories: difficulty and terrain (D/T). Both difficulty and terrain are rated using a five-point scale, with one star being the easiest and five stars the most difficult.

D/T on a Five-Point Scale

The interface on Geocaching. com makes each of these factors obvious. When you search for caches, look for the header (*D/T*) above the returned results. Using the five-point scale, a cache's difficulty rating might look like this: (1.2/4), where 1.2 rates the difficulty and 4 rates the terrain. In this example, finding the cache (1 point 2 out of 4) should be easy enough, provided you can actually get to its GPS coordinates.

D for Difficulty

Factors that increase the difficulty level for finding a geocache include the extent to which the cache is camouflaged, if special equipment (such as a flashlight) is needed, or if players need to solve a puzzle or overcome a challenge.

T for Terrain

Factors that increase the difficulty level for getting to the cache include the type of pathway that players must traverse (sidewalk, mountain trail, and so forth), the length of the walk (or hike), and if special equipment is needed (such as a four-wheel drive vehicle).

Into the Great Unknown

There you have it! You now know basically everything you need to go geocaching—a handheld GPS device, a compass, an account at Geocaching.com, and a list of caches to find. But before you stampede off into the great unknown, perhaps with a class in tow, I suggest you consider first what sort of skill you'd like your students to pick up along the way. To that end, I'd like to show you the many different types of caches, complete with details only hinted at thus far. I'd also like to impart some geocaching etiquette and strategies to ensure this game stays player friendly, relevant in terms of student education, and fun. In other words, before you go, please read the next chapter.

CHAPTER 3

Caching Your World: A Quick Tour

You have your GPS device in hand. You have a bank of cache waypoints and an account with Geocaching.com. You're ready to go geocaching. Excellent!

As you plot your first find, make sure your course for adventure passes through this chapter. In this chapter you will find:

- ▶ Greater detail about cache types: typical caches, puzzle caches, multi-caches, and virtual caches

- ▶ Advice on student-appropriate caches, including geocoins and travel bugs—student favorites

- ▶ A word or two about the artistry of finding, hiding, and describing a geocache

► Real-world advice for identifying and remedying problems, because every geocaching adventure should be an enjoyable experience

In Detail: Types of Geocaches

Geocaches come in a dizzying array of officially recognized types, many of which I touched on in the previous chapter. From traditional caches to puzzle caches, virtual caches to interactive caches—plus a variety in between—there's a cache type designed to appeal to you and every one of your students. That said, not all cache types are suited to classroom education. The types of caches outlined in this section are, at the very least, classroom-friendly. The extent to which you bring these cache types into your classroom is, of course, up to you.

Other Geocache Types

Cache types not covered in this section include bookcrossing and letterboxing. These cache types, as compelling, interesting, and classroom-friendly as they are, require unique preparations and props. To learn more about these geocaching activities refer to the section, "The World Wide Web: Finding Caches Near You" (page 34).

Traditional Cache

A traditional geocache consists of a few basic elements: A container (of any size, though preferably weatherproof), a logbook or log sheet, a pencil, and Stuff We All Get (SWAG). Traditional caches can be placed anywhere on Earth (they may not be buried) and are hidden in every imaginable way.

Container

Geocache containers are categorized by size: micro, small, regular, and large. (See pages 42–45 for a description and illustration of each.) A container is necessary only because a cache needs to contain a logbook. Anything with a watertight seal can be used as a container: film canister, breath mint box, plastic storage container, paint can, lawn gnome, ammo box, 55-gallon drum. … You name it.

Logbook/Log Sheet

This is the only item that really must be included in a geocache. A logbook or log sheet allows players to prove they found a cache—a posting on Geocaching.com is not enough. A logbook doesn't need to be a fancy, leather-bound artifact. It can be as simple as a scrap of paper. If the cache size allows, the hider of the cache should also include a writing instrument of some kind. Pencils are preferred because pen ink freezes in cold weather. A conscientious geocacher will tell players ahead of time to bring their own pen or pencil to the cache if it is too small to hold a pencil. Players who find a cache and sign its logbook still need to log the find on Geocaching.com to officially get credit for the find.

SWAG (Stuff We All Get)

In case you haven't already figured this out, the sport of
geocaching is more about the thrill of the hunt than it is about
striking it rich. Truth be told, the items found in a typical
geocache are of the cheap plastic trinket variety, the sort of stuff
that you'd find in a McDonald's Happy Meal. They're inexpensive,
durable, and fun—what's not to like? While I'm on the subject,
deep discount retailers are great places to get SWAG (Oriental
Trading Company, Dollar Tree, and their equivalents), as are
professional conferences, trade shows, and fairs. As you set out to
collect a swagbag full of McToys, you need to know that the "Take
One, Leave One" rule applies.

Take One, Leave One

The geocaching Rule of SWAG can be summed up with the axiom,
"Take One, Leave One." In other words, if you take an item out of a
cache you should put another item in its place. It's a type of trade.
And you should always make note of your activities in the cache's
logbook at Geocaching.com. As a common courtesy, players
should trade evenly or even trade up—if you take a heroic action
figure, don't leave a sticky bottle cap. Occasionally, geocachers
leave batteries as SWAG. This can be very helpful if your GPSr is
running low, so long as those batteries are fresh.

If players took things out of a cache and never put something in its
place, a lot of the game's fun would disappear. If part of geocaching's fun is finding new places and oddball treasures, the other part
is the satisfaction of sharing the secret places and curious artifacts
you've already discovered. Play fair. Take one, leave one.

Some items should never find their way into a geocache. These items include:

- Food items (no matter how well packaged)

- Knives, razors, or any other sharp objects

- Matches, fireworks, lighters, live ammo

- Drugs, alcohol, pornography, or other illicit material

- Any object or material that might harm a person who finds the cache

Trackable Items

Trackable items are one of the most exciting aspects of geocaching. The idea is simple. A small item is given a unique identifying code or tracking number. When that item enters the geocache stream, players log when and where they found that item, and when and where they placed it. The owner of that trackable item can follow the journey of that item via posts online. See the lesson plan "Where in the World Has Our Travel Bug Traveled?" in Part II of this book for ideas on bringing trackable items into your classroom.

Broadly speaking, the sport of geocaching features four types of trackables: geocoins, travel bugs, promotional items, and signature items. A gallery of trackables can be seen at www. geocaching.com/track/gallery.aspx. Trackable items do not all need to be purchased from the same place, but the places that sell them either need to coordinate the tracking numbers with Geocaching.com or provide their own system for tracking the items. A cottage industry has sprung up for people who like to create trackable items. CoinsAndPins is one such example (www.coinsandpins.com).

Geocoins

This is a catchall term that describes any item that can be tracked. While many geocoins are, in fact, coinlike in appearance, the physical similarities end there.

Players who find a geocoin are said to "grab" it when they visit the website associated with that particular geocoin (not all geocoins are tracked through Geocaching.com), and log that

FIGURE 3.1. A geocoin.

Photo courtesy of Flickr user Rev Dan Catt.

coin's tracking number. While online, players can upload photos of the geocoin they found and post comments regarding the find. The player then "holds" the coin (both in person and in an online inventory) until he or she drops that geocoin into another cache and logs the activity. All that's left is for another player to "grab" the coin and further its journey.

Confusion can arise if a player finds a geocoin, drops it into another cache, and is unable to log his or her activity *before* another player finds that same geocoin in its new location. Geocachers who wish to collect and distribute geocoins need to take the activity seriously.

Travel Bugs

Travel Bug is a registered trademark of Groundspeak. Travel bugs function exactly like geocoins. Shaped like a military dog tag, each travel bug (TB) is stamped with a unique serial number. Players attach a travel bug to another item and place the tagged item into a geocache. That item is called a "hitchhiker." Other players then pick up the hitchhiker and, like a geocoin, move it to other caches and log its progress.

The Golden Rule of Travel Bugs: Catch and Release

When you find a travel bug, the name of the game is catch and release. It is considered bad form to hold onto a travel bug for more than a few weeks. Moreover, when you find a travel bug and cast it back into the geo-stream, be sure to log the details of your activities online.

FIGURE 3.2. A travel bug and hitchiker.

Photo courtesy of Flickr user Stuant63.

Players are encouraged to write travel stories and take photos of the travel bug and its hitchhiker. Likewise, geocachers who create a travel bug are encouraged to create a specific goal for it. For example, a goal might be: I want a picture of my travel bug taken at the Great Wall of China.

Promotional Items

Created by companies like Groundspeak (the company that operates Geocaching.com), these trackable items are designed to promote the products and services of sponsor companies.

Promotional geocoins and travel bugs work in the same way as their noncommercial counterparts. Recent sponsors include Garmin and Jeep.

In fact, Jeep holds an annual geocaching event. In this case, Geocaching.com sends out travel bugs with little toy Jeep hitch-hikers to local geocaching groups, who distribute those travel bugs to their players. Geocaching.com doesn't profit from this effort—no money changes hands—but Jeep does gain exposure from the effort. Likewise, players don't win anything by finding and distributing these trackable items, though players can enter events like photo contests to win geocaching-related prizes. For more information about trackable items, visit the Trackable Items web page at Geocaching.com (www.geocaching.com/track).

Signature Items

In contrast to a generic McToy, a signature item is a tradable artifact that uniquely identifies a geocacher or geocaching team. A geocacher drops signature items into a cache to let other players know *I was here*. A signature item can be almost anything: trading cards, CDs, pins, buttons, patches, and the like. Players can make their own signature items, buy them from places like Dollar Tree, and customize them (or not). They can even purchase or create trackable items like custom-minted geocoins and travel bugs.

Both younger and older students enjoy creating their own signature items. This can lead to some compelling interdepartmental lessons and activities among the traditional classroom academic areas and the industrial, home, and fine arts departments; computer lab; vocational studies; and so on.

Puzzle Caches

A puzzle cache may or may not contain SWAG found in a traditional cache. Instead, it may contain coordinates to another cache, or a puzzle or riddle that, when solved, reveals the actual location of the cache prizes. Or something else; the possibilities are limited only by imagination.

See "A Week of Geocaching" in Chapter 1 for an example of a puzzle cache in action. Also consult the lesson plan "Pirate Treasure Maps" in Part II (page 107) for one way to bring a puzzle cache into your classroom.

Revelation by Encryption

On Geocaching.com, players can describe the caches they hide with witty word play and devious declarations. The site also allows them to post an encrypted clue. This encryption takes the form of a word scramble based on a simple letter-swapping rubric: A=N; B=O; C=P; and so on. Encrypting a clue is easy on Geocaching.com. Players simply enter the clue to be encrypted and the site does the rest.

The idea is not to confound prospective geocache seekers with a word scramble. Rather, the aim is to conceal what is likely to be a spoiler. Thus, decrypting the clue on Geocaching.com is as simple as clicking a button. True geocachers might print out an encrypted clue and take it with them, decrypting it in the field only if they absolutely cannot find the cache while at the correct GPS coordinates. It's not cheating. After you've hiked many rugged miles of forest trails and still can't find a cache, you might find yourself decrypting that clue, too.

Multi-Caches/Offset Caches

As the name implies, this cache type is actually a set of caches. It works like this: A first cache contains clues or coordinates to a second cache, which provides clues to a third cache, which provides clues to a fourth cache, and so on. Additionally, some of the caches in the chain can be virtual (i.e., instructions for using the virtual cache to continue the hunt would be posted on Geocaching.com). In geocaching lingo, this sort of virtual cache is called an "offset cache."

The catch is that only players who find the last cache in the chain are awarded credit for actually "finding" the cache. It can add up to many different and interesting stops. This type of cache is an excellent way to get students to visit a series of places, such as historical markers along Freedom Trail in Boston. I know of a multi-cache in California that, to find the final cache, requires players to find a cache in every county of the state. (I have heard of a family who has actually completed this particular multi-stage cache).

Virtual Caches, Webcam Caches, and EarthCaches

These types of caches are not contained in boxes that contain logbooks and SWAG, but are physical locations somewhere on Earth. The prize is finding the spot, and players get credit for finding this type of cache in any number of ways: by solving a puzzle, answering a set of questions specific to that location, or uploading a picture that somehow proves their find. These cache types are administered via the Waymarking.com and EarthCache.org websites.

Geocaching in the Park

Without a doubt, places like Yosemite National Park and Yellow-stone National Park are great places to go geocaching. And virtual caches make it possible—these are beautiful place best left as natural as possible. However, there are a number of state and local parks that have welcomed, even encouraged, cache placement to increase their number of visitors. Examples include the Ohio state parks and Lincoln City parks in Oregon, which even released their own geocoin!

In Yosemite National Park, there is a virtual cache located partway up Half Dome—one of the most famous hikes on one of the most famous rock formations in one of the most famous parks in the world. Once you get to the site of this virtual cache, you're asked a few questions such as, "How many stairs are beside you?" or "What do you see while standing on the x,y coordinate?" Once you get an Internet connection, you simply e-mail the answers to the person who set up that cache, who will give you credit for finding the cache.

A few things about virtual caches aren't necessarily obvious. You and your students need to know the questions for finding a virtual cache before you embark on the hunt. Print these out and take them with you. Along those lines, posting the answers about a virtual cache online will spoil that cache—anyone who reads the post will be able to get credit for the cache without ever actually finding it.

Virtual caches exist for a simple reason: A lot of locales don't allow physical caches, and some locations even expressly forbid them. National parks, for example, do not allow visitors to leave any unauthorized items within their boundaries. Virtual caches are not limited to parks. People don't really like to see strangers holding little electronic devices while stashing metal boxes in and around very public places like airports and shopping malls. The sport of geocaching makes the news every time a bomb squad is called in to blow up an ammo can under a bridge. Don't laugh—this has actually happened. You can probably guess what I'm going to say next: Stash caches responsibly, or go virtual.

See the lesson plan "Creating Virtual Geocaches" in Part II (page 126) for ideas on bringing virtual caches into your classroom.

To learn more about virtual caches, webcam caches, and EarthCaches, please review "The World Wide Web: Finding Caches Near You" in Chapter 2.

Wherigo: The Ultimate Virtual Multi-Cache

If ever there was a truly techie, location-specific geocaching activity, Wherigo is it. Imagine creating a multimedia game where players use GPS technology to move around in the real world but interact with virtual objects and characters. Imagine your students creating a Wherigo game that teachers, parents, and other students can use to explore your school or community via walking tours, puzzle games, and fictional adventures. Imagine that the software needed to create a Wherigo cartridge (game file) is a free, intuitive, downloadable Windows application.

Welcome to the world of Wherigo. The team that operates Geocaching.com also operates Wherigo, and they have gone out of their way to make this software as user-friendly as possible.

Great Wherigo Cartridges

You can play these Wherigo cartridges on your computer, for free. Go to the Wherigo Advanced Search web page (www.wherigo.com/search/AdvancedSearch.aspx) and do a keyword search for the following titles:

► J2B2: Village Robot. This is a fast-paced puzzle game that takes place at Seattle's Gasworks Park.

► The Arena. You are Captain Kirk, engaged in a battle of wits against the Gorn—as seen on the famous Star Trek episode "Arena"—set on location in Vasquez Rocks Park, California.

The Wherigo toolset contains a player and a builder application, both of which are free downloads from Wherigo.com. Users must create an account to access the content and services of Wherigo—it's free. Users can also sign in to Wherigo.com with an existing Geocaching.com account.

To play a Wherigo, users download a cartridge and load it onto a compatible GPS device, then go out and play. A cartridge directs players to a given GPS coordinate (or into a geographical zone), where the user must perform a task assigned by the game's creator. Like any other sort of virtual cache, Wherigo zones can exist anywhere on Earth—within the boundaries of a public park, on the grounds of a zoo or school, you name it. When players complete a task, the cartridge directs them to the next location within a zone (or to another zone) and the game continues. Players might meet fictional characters along the way or perform another task. In many respects, the game operates like an elaborate virtual multi-cache. But a great Wherigo cartridge, like a great cache, is more than the sum of its parts.

Because most players cannot travel to the exact location of every Wherigo adventure, Wherigo cartridges can also be played on a computer with a Windows operating system. This is done via an emulator—software that makes a second system (in this case, a computer) appear to work like the first system (in this case, a GPS device). In fact, an emulator is a perfect tool for playing Wherigo cartridges, especially if that cartridge takes place on the other side of the world. These cartridges are also a great source of inspiration for Wherigo builders, teachers, and students alike.

Wherigo-Compatible GPS Devices

Not all GPS devices can play a Wherigo cartridge. Most smartphones and pocket PCs are Wherigo compatible, as are a few newer Garmin GPS devices. Issues of hardware and software compatibility are moving targets. Thus, for the most current list of Wherigo-compatible devices, visit the Playing Wherigo section of the Wherigo website (www.wherigo.com/player/) and click on the links "Garmin handheld devices" and "GPS-enabled pocket PCs."

To build a Wherigo cartridge, users download the Wherigo Builder Application and set to work. Building a cartridge is a straightforward process, accomplished via three essential steps: mapping zones, creating a story, and sharing it online. It's a bit more complicated than this, of course. Luckily, Wherigo provides an online tutorial that will guide you and your students through the basics of creating a Wherigo cartridge. Users will also have access to a FAQ and a number of other key resources. Look for Building Cartridges with Wherigo at Wherigo.com (www. wherigo.com/builder/). For more advice on bringing the Wherigo experience into your classroom, please see lesson plan "Real World RPG" in Chapter 5.

The Art and Science of Finding Geocaches

A long journey toward finding a geocache does not begin with a physical first step. For most, it begins with an Internet search on the official site and database for the game of geocaching— Geocaching.com. But this is not always the case, especially for teachers with a classroom of students.

Geocaching in Education: Finding Caches without Geocaching.com

As heretical as this may sound, I recommend that teachers who want to lead a class on geocaching adventures forego the caches found on Geocaching.com, at least to start. There are a few good reasons for this. First and foremost, geocaching in education is not about simply taking students to a site and turning them loose to find SWAG. For educators, geocaching should supplement existing curricula in a meaningful way.

For students, geocaching should be an engaging activity that makes their world a little bigger and a lot more interesting. This is why I recommend that teachers introduce geocaching as a purely school- or class-based activity. Students should learn the process of finding and creating geocaches through tried-and-true instructional methods like modeling, guided practice, and perhaps a culminating activity. During this process, students and teachers alike can use the Geocaching.com website for useful examples regarding cache types, creating clues, and posting finds. After students have demonstrated mastery of the entire process (and the desire to do more geocaching), teachers can take the class on a Geocaching.com-inspired field trip.

Finally, every classroom teacher should know that when someone creates a geocache and posts it to Geocaching.com, that geocache must meet a few basic criteria. For more information about these criteria, see "Listing Guidelines for Geocaching.com" on page 89. Also see the lesson plans in Chapter 5 for a range of classroom-based geocaching activities that neither call for nor require access to Geocaching.com.

Before introducing the Geocaching.com site to your students, you should be thoroughly familiar with a few key areas of the website.

Zip Code Search

The typical search on Geocaching.com is done by zip code. A zip code search will return a list of all caches within and around the zip code you enter—a 100-mile radius can easily return hundreds of pages and thousands of caches. Each entry includes cache type, size, post-date, difficulty, and so forth. You can peruse a list of results to find specific types of geocaches that interest you. While looking through the list of results, you can sort geocaches by their proximity to a specific location (such as your school building or field trip site). Figure 3.3 shows a zip code search.

FIGURE 3.3. A "search by zip code" results page.

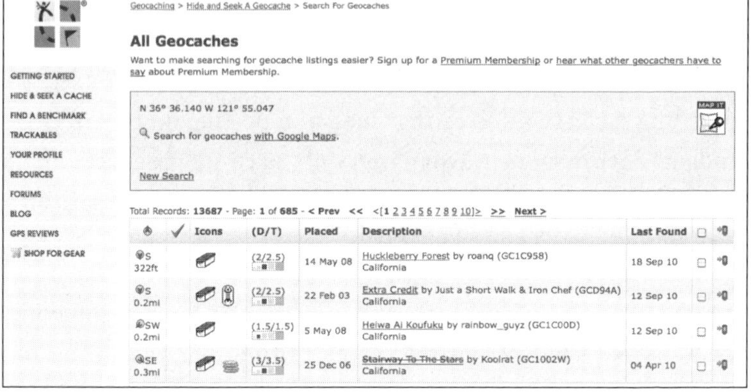

Your search can also be done via Google Maps, which is embedded in Geocaching.com. By clicking on the Google Maps option, you can narrow your results to see geocaches (waypoints) layered over Google Maps itself (Figure 3.4). As you pan the map, or zoom in and out, the waypoints will regenerate accordingly. A sidebar that contains more information about each visible cache also refreshes in real time. It's simply a great feature.

FIGURE 3.4. A Google Map search, with waypoints.

Geocaching.com also offers a downloadable Google Earth layer that can be used to find geocaches. With the Geocaching layer enabled, any search in Google Earth will reveal geocaches hidden near specific street addresses or landmarks.

No matter the method you use to search for caches, there are important factors to consider, especially with students.

Cache Details

Geocaching.com provides easy-to-identify information about each cache on the results page: cache type, contents, size, D/T (difficulty and terrain), date placed, a brief description, and the last few log entries from geocachers who have searched for the cache.

FIGURE 3.5. A cache details page.

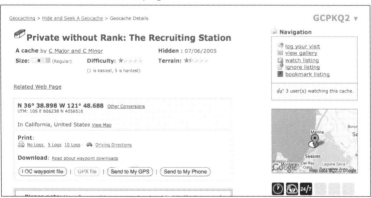

As you click from the search results page to a cache details page (Figure 3.5), there are a number of items to consider in terms of its appropriateness for you and your students. With this in mind, look for the attributes box (located on the right side of the page).

FIGURE 3.6. A cache attributes box.

The individual who placed the cache should have provided details about the cache and its surrounding area. The at-a-glance icons in the Figure 3.6 attributes box will tell you if stealth is required to find the cache, its availability in inclement (winter) weather, hours of availability (24/7), how long it should take you to find it (less than an hour), if the cache is kid friendly, parking availability, and other relevant information regarding permissions, conditions, equipment required, hazards, and facilities.

If it's so far, so good, look farther down the cache details page. The creator of the geocache should have also included a (hopefully fun) description of the cache, and possibly an encrypted hint for finding the cache. Finally, the bottom of this page will likely feature log notes from geocachers who have recently tried to find that particular cache. These log notes can provide additional tips about the location or condition of that geocache (Figure 3.7). (BTW, TFTC means *Thanks for the cache*.)

Now that you've got a list of caches just waiting to be found, how are you going to remember the details of each cache after you leave your desk and hit the trail (or turn off your laptop, or lose your WiFi connection)? Wouldn't it be great if you could take your treasure maps with you? You can!

FIGURE 3.7. Cache log notes page.

Going Old School: Printer, Paper, Pen, and Clipboard
==

The most straightforward way to keep track of prospective caches is the most obvious. As outlined previously, each cache on Geocaching.com has a dedicated Cache Details page. To take your chosen cache clues with you, simply print out the cache details page for every prospective cache (or copy and paste this information into a Word or Excel file). This could also become a "reading for information" activity for students, for which they must analyze content, predict what sort of materials they need in the field, what they expect the cache to be (or not be), and so on. Existing posts on Geocaching.com offer excellent models for students when they go about creating clues for caches of their own making. See "The Art and Science of Hiding Geocaches," page 82.

Gathering cache information this way can be a labor-intensive process. It might get expensive in terms of printer ink and paper.

Plus you'll need to organize what can easily become a mound of paperwork and take a lot of prep time. This means staples, clipboards, folders, or three-ring binders. Moreover, you or your students will have to manually enter the GPS coordinates for each cache into each GPS device (watch for mistakes), take those papers on the hunt, make notes on them, and keep them safe long enough to log your activities on Geocaching.com.

This method, tried and true as it is, begs for improvement. One method for improving this process is to use a GPSr that connects to a computer. (See "PC Interface" on page 28.) Or you can go paperless.

Going Paperless: A Triumph of Technology

Thanks to the advent of pocket PCs (handhelds) and smart-phones (including iPhone, Blackberry, and Android), users can access Geocaching.com from any location at any time. Obtaining geocache information on the fly is a huge boon. Without a smart-phone or a pocket PC, geocachers have to log on to Geocaching.com to download and print out geocache information (waypoints, hints, etc.) before going on a hunt.

But with a smartphone or pocket PC, users don't need to plan ahead. They need only to log on to Geocaching.com from wher-ever they happen to be, let the geocaching software determine their current location and download the geocaches nearest them, and they're off. Android smartphones and iPhones can also act as their GPSr.

If you would like to try paperless geocaching without having to pay for a wireless plan, there are many software programs that give you the ability to put information from Geocaching.com onto iPods and PDAs. For more information about this type of paperless geocaching visit the Geocaching Software section on the Geocaching website (www.geocaching.com/waypoints). For an overview of smartphones and geocaching, see "Tools of the Trade: Popular GPS Receivers" in Chapter 2.

With all of your geocaching eggs in one fragile, high-tech basket, you'll want to vigorously guard that basket. Issues like device durability and battery life should factor heavily in your decisions. This is to say that when you go paperless, don't forget to pack a pencil and some paper.

The Hunt

Now that you are completely outfitted for geocaching, it's time to find a few official geocaches. An outdoor adventure like the following is, in essence, a geocaching inservice activity. As you will recall, here are the basic steps for a Geocache.com hunt:

1. Select a geocache from Geocaching.com.

2. Enter the geocache coordinates into your handheld GPSr.

3. Use your GPSr to locate the geocache.

4. Find the cache, sign the logbook, and trade SWAG (if applicable).

5. Visit Geocaching.com and log your find.

Sounds easy, right? Well, let's take a look at some of the geocaches I recently set out to find. I have included the unique Geocaching Code (GC Code) for the following caches. When you enter a GC Code on Geocaching.com, you will be taken directly to the details page of that particular cache. The code shown in Figure 3.5 (upper-right corner) is GCPKQ2.

The hunt for GC Code GC1KKWE (Figures 3.8–3.10)

FIGURE 3.8. A tranquil park can be home to a treasure chest of fun.

FIGURE 3.9. When looking for a cache, one clue might be an unusual pile of rocks or sticks.

FIGURE 3.10. Finding this size cache usually means interesting prizes for your students.

The hunt for GC Code GC1C74X (Figures 3.11–3.13)

FIGURE 3.11. Double-check your coordinates before you set out to find the cache.

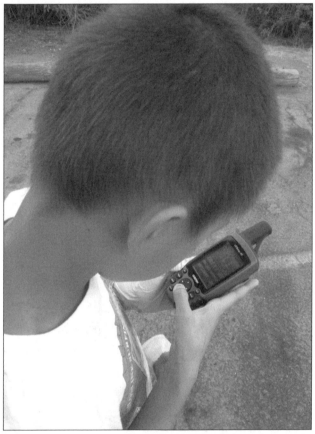

FIGURE 3.12. Many times a cache will not be hidden at eye level.

FIGURE 3.13. Happiness is a found geocache.

The hunt for GC Code GC1X3DX (Figures 3.14–3.16)

FIGURE 3.14. Geocaches can be found in the most unlikely places.

FIGURE 3.15. Sometimes caches are hidden in plain sight.

FIGURE 3.16. Not much room for SWAG, but finding a cache like this will make a student feel like a spy.

The Art and Science of Hiding Geocaches

Perhaps the only thing more fun than finding geocaches is creating and hiding geocaches. Spend any time hunting for geocaches and you'll quickly recognize when another player put a lot of thought and cunning into creating and hiding a cache—and when a player did little more than follow shopworn conventions.

Advice Online

Geocaching.com features good, basic, and commonsense advice for hiding caches. This advice resides on a single page, and its brevity equates to easy accessibility for students:

Go to Geocaching.com > Hiding Your First Geocache (www.Geocaching.com/about/hiding.aspx).

Geocaching.com also posts clear, continually updated requirements and guidelines about hiding caches. If your cache fails to meet any of these requirements or guidelines, the operators of this website won't post your cache details—or will quickly "archive" it into oblivion after other geocachers post complaints. (Rest assured, they will.)

Finally, Geocaching.com does not post so-called "temporary" or "private party" caches. For this reason, classroom-specific caches placed on school grounds are not appropriate for Geocaching.com. For these exclusive caches, worksheets and other printouts work extremely well.

Because these rules and regulations continually change as the game evolves, simply direct your web browser to Geocaching.com to see the latest. Go to Geocaching.com > Listing Guidelines (www.Geocaching.com/about/guidelines.aspx) to review updates.

To keep the sport of geocaching interesting and challenging, both for you and your students, I encourage you to create and hide caches with all the unbridled creativity and devious glee that you can muster.

As a treasure maker, you create a camouflaged container, select the treasure your cache will contain, and select a location to stash your cache. Then you must entice other players to hunt for your newly placed geocache by providing clever hints and GPS coordinates. Easy enough, right?

When you create a geocache, remember that you are asking someone to take time out of his or her one-and-only life to hunt around for an item you put into the world. So before you throw some junk into a plastic sandwich bag, toss it under a bush, and call it a geocache, ask yourself a few basic questions: What sort of cache would educators and students find worth pursuing? What sort of cache fits with my curriculum? What sort of location would interest me and my students? While you're at it, think about the caches that did not appeal to you (and won't appeal to your students), or worse, wasted your time or were dangerous to pursue. Likewise, consider the caches and locations that you thoroughly enjoyed. Create your geocaches accordingly.

The Art of the Cache

A great cache possesses that "certain something." It might be its setting—a lonely mountaintop with a sweeping vista that spreads magnificently to the horizon, or above the trophy case in a hallway filled to overflowing with noise and bustling bodies. It might be its container and its placement—a custom-made container that perfectly fits into its hiding spot. Or it might be in its difficulty to find—the cunning of a good puzzle married to a challenging pursuit that culminates when both puzzle and pursuit fuse into a glorious ah-ha! moment.

The possibilities go on and on. Like great art—art that draws us in, toys with our expectations, then surprises us with a rush of insight—a great cache inspires, outrages, and ultimately delights us. A great cache creates a memorable experience. A great cache is great fun. Examples abound on Geocaching.com. Water displacement caches are particularly enjoyable. One I recommend is Liquid Sunshine (GCJ2CQ). The cache is easy to get to (if you are in Portland, Oregon) and fun to find. Players need precisely 67.6 ounces of water to raise this cache.

Sometimes good caches go bad. Geocaches that were well hidden or looked very nice in the beginning do not always age well. For example, caches wrapped with canvas or decorated with cloth flowers from a craft shop do not last very long when left to the elements.

While not everyone can create great, weather-resistant art, I believe that anyone can create a great cache. The crucial ingredients are practice and the desire to improve at the craft. You must hunt for caches and then study the caches you find. If you want to create great caches I recommend that you hunt for at least a handful of caches before you go about hiding caches or leading a class in this activity. Not only will you discover some good caches (and probably some good caches gone bad), but you'll get a sense of the sort of caches that appeal to you. For the educator, creating a great cache is akin to creating a great lesson.

As you seek caches, building your knowledge base and finding inspiration, I believe you will discover a few key elements shared by all great caches: a great journey, an appropriate location, an accurate description, and good site maintenance.

The Journey

One of the true pleasures of geocaching is going to places you wouldn't otherwise even think of going. No matter how many places you've visited, how many miles you've hiked, a new trail, a new town, a new street always beckons. And what holds true for you holds true for your students. But geocaching isn't an exercise in random adventure. The sport of geocaching provides players a reason for going to new, and sometimes strange, places. This is the very definition of adventure.

To create a great cache, start by creating a good adventure. Carefully consider where you're sending your prospective geocache hunters. Will the journey provide excitement? Will it open up a curious new world, heretofore only known to a select few? This journey can take the form of a stroll around the school grounds, a foray down the block, a challenging hike, some great scenery, even better views, and a startling find. Will this cache be worth the time it takes to create it? Will it be worth the time and attention of your students? Will your cache enhance the progression of your existing curriculum? Will it offer new ways to approach old materials? Let me put it this way: If you went hunting for your cache, would it be worth *your* time?

If you create a geocache adventure for your students, consider more than their abilities and temperaments. Great caches entail a journey that enhances and illuminates your existing curriculum and even helps students to become better, more informed citizens of your community.

Location

A cache can be located almost anywhere. Any public setting—no matter how wild or urban—can provide great cache hunting grounds. That's one of the magical realities of geocaching. My advice is simple: Select hiding locations that are challenging and interesting, no matter the setting. Choose a container and SWAG that somehow emphasizes, enhances, or enriches the location you choose. This vessel will put your cache in harmony with its environment, even if it's in a minor key. As for the hiding spot itself, the best caches are those that are hidden in plain sight. Players delight in finding caches like this. Strive to give players that most delicious moment of discovery—the moment when they say, "Oh, of course!"

As an aside, putting a cache in a dangerous place does not heighten the experience—it simply puts someone in harm's way. No caches alongside train tracks or attached to electrical boxes—or inserted inside of them. The same goes for appropriateness. No ammo cans on school property or outside of police stations. No caches in environmentally sensitive areas, on historical sites, or on private property (without permission).

Accuracy

For some geocachers, accuracy means research—careful environmental assessments, sampling and cross-sampling waypoints—and obsessive attention to detail: finding the perfect container (not just a good one, the *perfect* one), and an impeccable assortment of SWAG.

Waypoint accuracy is a critical component in the making of a great cache. To get an accurate GPS measurement for the location of your cache, you need to take many sample readings from many different spots. The best publically available GPSr is accurate only up to 10 feet (3 meters). Take the time, take good notes, do the math, and do this right. Your lesson, and your students, will benefit immeasurably when you pay attention to this seemingly trivial detail.

Likewise, are the cache details you provide to your students accurate? How accurate? This goes beyond the waypoint coordinates. Will your clues make sense to your students when they arrive at the cache location? Of course, you shouldn't give away the exact location of your cache; that's no fun. On the other hand, if you leave out a critical piece of information that, in effect, makes finding the cache impossible (or highly unlikely), that's not fun. That's infuriating.

Maintenance

Once you create a cache, it's your responsibility to maintain it. This is particularly relevant long term for caches posted on Geocaching.com, but it also applies to caches that exist for a single lesson. Being responsible for a cache means monitoring student feedback regarding each cache. It means periodically retrieving the cache to make sure all is in proper order. Great caches are well maintained. To this end, I recommend that you make cache maintenance an easy thing to do. Hide your caches in places you frequent during your daily or weekly routine. Keep it simple.

The Art of the Post

You may have created a great cache. In fact, you know that you've created a great cache. But until you tell others about your cache, it may as well not exist. An individual's first encounter with your cache will be the cache details you reveal, be it on an in-class worksheet or a cache details page on Geocaching.com. Thus, the greatness of your cache begins with the clues you create.

Post Fright—Fear of Posting

People new to geocaching often discover that writing information about their cache is more difficult than finding the most deviously hidden cache. For teachers accustomed to creating worksheets and assignments, this may not be a daunting task. But for adults of a certain generation, posting a set of details to a website may represent a first attempt at online publishing. This can be unnerving for them. Students who have grown up "wired" may not have these fears exactly—their challenge may be in unlearning bad habits developed through hours of instant messaging and texting to friends.

As with all lessons that ultimately promote classroom publishing, guide your students carefully through the process. Monitor not only what students say and how they say it, but also how they feel about creating and publishing their posts. Do they feel free to express themselves, or are they afraid of making mistakes or worried about the reactions of their peers?

Cache details should honestly and accurately reflect what you've hidden—in a fun and compelling way that piques the interest of your students and aligns with your lesson. Think of your cache details as being a promise that your cache will deliver upon. Each promise, then, requires its own sensibility. My advice is that you read a lot of cache details postings on Geocaching.com—from all over the country and around the world. You may never endeavor to find those caches; the point is to understand how others have touted their caches.

When describing your cache, sometimes a straightforward approach is best. Sometimes clever clue-laden wordplay is the way to go. Sometimes a puzzle game is your most effective strategy (see "A Week of Geocaching" in Chapter 1). Tease your readers; reveal just enough to make the hunt interesting without spoiling the surprises that you have so carefully laid in wait.

Listing Guidelines for Geocaching.com

Although posting a details cache page on Geocaching.com is free, it is not a free-for-all. Before a cache details page is posted, a volunteer at Groundspeak reviews the posting request for accuracy, completeness, and compliance with the guidelines. This process can take some time. Plan accordingly.

As I noted earlier, Geocaching.com does not post temporary or private party caches. Official geocaches must be available for at least three months and be accessible to anyone who visits the site. This means that, as far as Geocaching.com is concerned, caches intended for one-day events on private property cannot be included in its database. Caches intended for classroom use on school grounds are not appropriate for Geocaching.com.

This doesn't mean you can't create your own geocaching events, it just means the postings for these types of events won't appear on Geocaching.com. For temporary caches intended for day-to-day use in class, worksheets and printouts work extremely well.

To see the latest listing guidelines, please go to Geocaching.com > Listing Guidelines (www.geocaching.com/about/guidelines.aspx).

Posting a Cache

OK. You created a great cache. You've reviewed the regulations and guidelines—your cache is good to go. You've written the teaser text for your cache details page. Now what? Why, post it, of course. Geocaching.com makes it very, very easy for you to do this. Simply go to the Report/Edit a Cache page at Geocaching. com, fill in the blanks, and send it in (www.geocaching.com/hide/report.aspx).

For security reasons, you only have 40 minutes to fill out and submit a Report/Edit a Cache page. After 40 minutes, your session will expire, and you'll lose all the information you've so laboriously entered. A word to the wise: preview the Report/Edit a Cache page before you enter any information. Log off the website and write your cache details in a word processing program. Then log back in to the website and copy and paste your text into the appropriate fields. If you make some mistakes, don't worry. The owner of the cache can always edit the cache's description.

◄ PART II ►

Geocaching in the Classroom and Beyond

A lesson on geocaching can be something as simple as a class hour spent hunting for caches on the school grounds. Alternatively, the lesson can be an elaborate interdisciplinary experience that features mathematics, cartography, geology, ecology, language arts, industrial arts, computer programming, physical education, field trips, and a unit-culminating project.

Geocaching is a dynamic activity, and the lessons and ideas presented here aim to reflect that. Rather than a catalog of lesson plans and worksheets, Part II of this book is a primer.

Part II is intended to help you:

- ▸ Prepare to bring geocaching into your classroom

- ▸ Determine what skills students should acquire

- ▸ Present the concept of geocaching to your colleagues

These elements and accompanying lesson plans will help you:

- ▸ Create lessons that feature geocaching

- ▸ Use geocaching to support your existing curriculum

- ▸ Lead your students on educational geocaching adventures designed to capture their imaginations

CHAPTER 4

Geocaching across the Curriculum

The creativity and real-world problem solving involved in creating and finding geocaches are a natural fit across grade levels and subject areas. Now that you have an understanding of what geocaching is all about, and what sort of treasures and pitfalls await, you're ready to incorporate GPS and geocaching into your curriculum.

In this chapter you will find:

- ▶ Real-world preparation basics

- ▶ Advice on lesson design

- ▶ A discussion of the role of online maps and podcasting in geocaching

Real-World Preparations

The sort of preparations you need to make before taking a class geocaching depends upon a multitude of variables: the sort of instructional unit you're teaching, how the activity of geocaching is integrated into your lessons, the size of your class or group, the type and number of GPS receivers you have, the availability of Internet-ready technologies at school, the volume and type of caches you plan to find or hide, the location(s) of those caches, the season, and weather. The same can be said about the equipment and items you and your students might need: rain gear, boots, hats, sunscreen, sunglasses, gloves, backpacks, spare batteries and chargers, first-aid kits, allergy meds, insect repellents, snacks, trade SWAG, and so on.

If you are new to geocaching, keep it simple until you figure out the types of caches you enjoy finding (or hiding) and you have a good grasp on using your GPSr. I recommend that you reflect on how you prepare for a geocaching expedition yourself: Do you typically prepare meticulously for a weekend adventure, or do you dash out for a quick find over the lunch hour? After you've had a chance to audit the world of geocaching, you'll have a good sense of the lessons you will want to create for your students, and how you'll go about bringing those lessons to life.

While I'm on the subject of the real world, what follows are essentials that apply to any geocaching expedition:

> ► Carefully audit every potential geocaching location prior
> to taking students there. Is it safe? How safe? What extra
> equipment and tools will students need? How much time is
> required for travel to the location and back? How much time

will students have to actually go geocaching? Are bathroom facilities available? Where? Can you monitor all of your students, or do you have enough adult volunteers to help out?

▶ Tell somebody where you are going. This seems obvious. (This point is no doubt more applicable for home-schooled students than for students who attend school in a more public setting.) Certainly, most day hikes don't turn into emergency situations, but one misstep and an otherwise well-planned day can take a nasty turn. Hikers (hence, geocachers) have come up with various self-preservation measures: contacting friends and family prior to the trip; checking in with park rangers before hitting the trail; and placing clearly visible placards in their parked cars that reveal who they are, what they are doing, when they started their journey, when they plan to return, and even where they are headed and how they plan to get there (these plac- ards can include vehicle/owner contact information, cell phone numbers, GPS coordinates of the cache, and even a cache's unique ID number). Extreme? Maybe, but it is better to be safe than sorry.

▶ Be aware of your surroundings. Stress to students that they need to look up from their GPS receivers as they hunt for caches. Have students geocache in pairs—one to look out, the other to work the GPSr—or in small groups. Every experienced geocacher has a painful story that involves an immovable object (tree, rock, ravine, light post, car), a GPSr, a nearby cache, and a lapse in attention. Don't let your students take home their own version of this story!

The Kid in All of Us

For younger students geocaching is all about the SWAG. It's all about knowing that secret treasures exist and are just waiting to be found.

Older students and adults are, of course, more sophisticated. The SWAG probably won't capture their imaginations so much as will the prospect of stepping into a secret world that's hidden in plain view. In this regard, it's a real-world Harry Potter adventure. It is no accident that non-geocachers are known as "muggles" (nonmagic folk).

Geocaching lore is rife with stories about players who camouflage themselves to look official and otherwise beyond reproach. Geocachers have been known to carry clipboards and wear hardhats. Some even play dress-up—pressed green gabardine for parks; suits and ties (and hardhats!) for urban adventure. Part of the fun is hiding in plain sight, just like the caches themselves.

If you play dress-up, remember to play responsibly: No stashing caches in our National Parks or trespassing on private property. Do not play in public places with items like ammo boxes—not only can genuine trouble ensue for you and your school, but you'll be giving the game of geocaching a bad reputation that it doesn't deserve.

Of course, when a full class is unleashed on a geocaching expedition, the "secret world" aspect of the game is moot. But the other powers of geocaching will remain: the pleasure of the hunt, the dazzle of the technology, and the glimmer of hidden SWAG. Do it right, and your students will learn a lot more than what the lesson objectives prescribe.

▶ Plan for breaks. Students caught up in the excitement of the hunt may not take time out to hydrate or review information vital to the hunt. Break time gives you time to assess how well you and your students are holding up physically, the extent to which everyone is staying on task, and so on.

The more prepared you and your support staff are, and the better prepared your students are, the more enjoyable the experience will be for everyone.

Five Steps to Get Your Classroom Geocaching

Taking yourself, or a friend or two, out on a geocaching expedition is one thing, but a whole class is another matter entirely. While I can't possibly cover every issue that an educator and class might encounter, I can provide some field-tested advice for classroom-sized geocaching expeditions.

1. **Create a Standard Geocaching Kit**
   It is easiest to teach students about geocaching if everybody uses the same equipment. Try to set up each team of students with the same type of GPSr, some gloves, a flashlight, and a pencil.

2. **Create Classroom Experts**
   Every classroom has some students who are naturally gifted with gadgets. Gather these students and teach them how to use the classroom GPS receivers. As you teach the class how to geocache, these students can be the guides to help all of the students get accustomed to the equipment.

3. **Get a Bird's-Eye View**

   Before you set out to find your geocaches, show your class the area that you will be searching on Google Maps or Google Earth. This will help them identify landmarks and set parameters while they search.

4. **You Don't Need to Stay on the Published Path**

   By no means do you and your class need to limit yourselves to geocaches published at Geocaching.com. Set waypoints at interesting or important points on your school campus. Ask students to find these waypoints in addition to answering questions or using the waypoints in a story.

5. **Geocaching is a Team Activity**

   Geocaching is an ideal activity for cooperative learning. Not every student needs to hold the GPSr for every find. Form geocaching teams and ask one student to keep track of important details about the cache being hunted; ask another student to decipher the clue for the cache, should it be needed; ask another student to input the coordinates into the GPSr and keep the team headed in the right direction. Rotate the tasks for each geocache.

Lesson Design

While GPS technology itself is ever-changing, the sensibilities of great lessons that incorporate geocaching are constant.

Determine What Your Students Should Learn

What your students should learn will inform how you bring geocaching into your classroom. Simply, what do you want geocaching to do for your students? Do you want this activity primarily to:

▶ Guide student learning about the larger world? (geography, geology, ecology, history, etc.)

▶ Make abstract concepts real? (mathematics, physics, chemistry)

▶ Help students improve logic and problem-solving skills? (solving puzzles, finding caches)

▶ Practice community etiquette and promote small-group work? (online and the real world)

▶ Provide focus for writing and art assignments (posting online, creating signature items)

▶ Something else?

It goes without saying that you will align your geocaching lessons to your state and district standards and curricula. Likewise, you will no doubt provide students with clear expectations, guidance, practice, goals, and outcomes. Look to the lesson plans in Chapter 5 for inspiration as you create your own activities.

Make the Abstract Concrete

The underlying concepts that make GPS work—electricity, longitude/latitude, and satellite triangulation—are abstract concepts.

As educators, we know that many students have trouble with intangibles. Under the guise of geocaching, abstract concepts can be made concrete for students. Using a GPSr and a few simple handouts, for example, concepts like "true north" and "magnetic north" can be explained, demonstrated, and applied to the real world in one seamless sweep.

Concepts like satellite triangulation are more difficult to make "real" in the classroom, but it can be done. I heard about a very clever educator who hid a cache in his classroom, taped up pictures of satellites in the classroom, and used lengths of string to demonstrate relative distances from each satellite to the cache, and thereby "triangulated" the cache. This also doubled as a neat trigonometry lesson. The magic of GPS technology thus made real, the class then went outside to hunt for caches on school grounds. Websites like CyberBee (www.cyberbee.com/gps_sites.html) exist to help you bring abstract concepts like triangulation into your classroom.

Educate Your Fellow Educators

Geocaching is one of those rare activities that transcends the divisions among traditional subject areas. It also provides educators a way to focus their subject matter. If you catch the geocaching bug, spread it to your fellow educators without reservation.

> **Math teachers** can use geocaching and GPS to make abstract concepts real and relevant (e.g., what a degree is in relation to miles).

> **Science teachers** can use geocaching to give shape to inquiries into the natural world.

Language Arts teachers can use geocache logbooks and online posts to give focus to student writing (take a look at the Geocaching.com post Double Dog Dare–GC10H56).

Social Studies teachers can use trackable items to help students explore other cultures.

Physical Education teachers can use geocaching to promote outdoor adventure.

Art teachers can use geocaching to guide student projects via the creation and release of travel bugs and signature items.

From Muggle to Magical

The world comprises two types of people: those who know about the magic of geocaching and those who don't. A fun way to introduce younger students to geocaching is to designate them "muggles." Before conducting a classroom-based geocaching expedition, students can wear a small item that assigns them to muggle status—a pin, patch, sticker, and the like. Then, after a student finds his or her first cache, the muggle item can be swapped for an item that features a lightning bolt, indicating their graduation from muggle status.

Maps That Enhance Geocaching

Geocaching can add a great deal to learning activities; however, there are a few limitations that can be mitigated by using other technology, such as Google Maps and Google Earth. First, because GPS receivers cannot receive signals from GPS satellites while indoors, geocaching is primarily an outdoor activity. Because it is an outdoor activity, it is very susceptible to change due to weather. In the event that a geocaching activity is planned but cannot be completed, Google Earth or Google Maps can be used by students to identify significant landmarks. Unlike using printed maps, students are not limited to merely viewing content. Students can add content to Google Earth through placemarks or image overlays, or they can use Google Maps to view geocache locations.

Also, some locations have a more historically rich geocaching landscape than others. For example, downtown Boston is very different in this regard from the central valley of California. It is unlikely that all students can geocache along Freedom Trail in Boston, so this is a perfect opportunity to use Google Earth or Google Maps to bring Freedom Trail into the classroom. Beyond being able to point out parts of Freedom Trail to students, teachers can ask students to explain the historical significance of specific locations on Freedom Trail by adding placemarks, text, and embedded images and videos.

You may feel that previewing the location of geocaches with tools such as Google Maps or Google Earth is cheating. In terms of geocaching in education, it isn't. This software not only provides a bird's-eye view of cache locations, it also adds a great deal to lessons that involve maps, history, or geocaches. Instead of only looking at locations on wall maps, teachers and students can interact with geography using Google Maps and Google Earth.

Google Maps

Creating interactive Google Maps requires either a Google account or a Gmail account. Logging into Google Maps with one of these accounts allows students to work collaboratively with you and their peers to create interactive maps. These maps can pinpoint points of interest added by the students—text, images, links to websites, and even embedded video clips. After creating a Google Map, students can make it available for the rest of the class to view. Students can also create a portable version of the map that anybody can open with Google Earth.

Google Earth

Google Earth is popular because of the numerous layers that add information to the satellite imagery of the globe. For example, teachers and students can turn on layers that show images from around the world, or even recent earthquake activity around the globe. Students do not need to have a Google or Gmail account in order to add their own layer of information to Google Earth. By adding placemarks and paths, students can retrace historical journeys or their geocaching journeys as a layer on Google Earth. Students can also add image layers in Google Earth that overlay the satellite images with pictures from their digital cameras or other image resources.

Podcasting Gives Geocaching a Voice

GPS satellite signals do not travel well through ceilings and walls, so one of the limitations to traditional geocaching is that it must be done outdoors. Technology such as Google Maps, Google Earth, and podcasting all provide ways for students to continue geocaching activities while indoors. Podcasts are audio recordings that are simple to create with a digital voice recorder. These voice recordings can either be created by the teacher to provide further information about a geocache, or created by students to provide their descriptions or responses to questions provided by a geocache.

A great extension to a geocaching activity is to set coordinates that will bring students to a specific location, then ask them to listen to a recording on an MP3 player that provides verbal directions to finish locating the geocache. Adding a podcast to a geocaching activity means that students can be directed to find an indoor geocache. To some geocachers, this type of activity has become known as a "podcache." For more information about geocaching and podcaches, visit the PodCacher website (www.podcacher.com).

CHAPTER 5

Lesson Plans

These lessons are designed to illustrate how geocaching can be incorporated into classroom studies. I trust that you will tailor these lessons to suit your particular teaching style, academic environment, and curriculum.

Beginning Geocaching Lessons

- ► Pirate Treasure Maps (Grades 1–4, ages 5–10)

- ► Classroom Geocache (Grades 4–6, ages 8–12)

- ► Transplants (Grades 6–8, ages 10–14)

Intermediate Geocaching Lessons

► Where in the World Has Our Travel Bug Traveled? (Grades 3–5, ages 7–11)

► Real World RPG (Grades 9–12, ages 13–18)

Enhanced Geocaching Lessons

These lessons use additional technologies.

► What Season Is It? (Grades 6–8, ages 10–14)

► Creating Virtual Geocaches (Grades 6–8, ages 10–14)

► Geocaching Podcasts (Grades 6–8, ages 10–14)

► Podcache Audio Tours (Grades 9–12, ages 13–18)

Beginning Geocaching Lesson

Pirate Treasure Maps
Language Arts, Mathematics, Art
Grade Levels 1–4 (ages 5–10)

Description

Students will hunt for treasure via a multistage cache.

Objective

Students will learn about the cardinal directions and how to use technology (compasses, maps, GPS) to navigate.

Materials

GPS receivers, pens or pencils and paper, compasses, various art supplies

Preparation

Prior to the lesson, educator will:

1. Seed an outdoor area with two sets of three intermediary "treasure" containers (for a total of six) that students will find, and (at least) one "final" treasure container. The first set of intermediary containers should contain clues for finding a container in the second set, and each container in the second set should contain a clue for finding a "final" treasure container.

2. Input two intermediate waypoints (first set and second set), and one "final" waypoint into GPS receivers. Each GPSr will thereby contain a different "pathway" to finding the final treasure. If no GPS receivers are available, waypoints can be provided on paper (students will need a compass to guide them).

3. Create a blank "treasure map" template that each student will receive. This template should contain the basic geographical landmarks of the hunting grounds, though with plenty of room for students to add in their own important landmarks and artistic flourishes.

4. Provide students with instruction on the concepts of cardinal directions, using compasses, deciphering maps, guided practice for working out the sorts of clues/puzzles they will encounter during the hunt, and using a GPSr (if applicable).

Procedures

1. After instructing students on the proper use and responsibilities of the treasure hunt itself and on using technologies like a GPSr, give each student a blank "treasure" map and group the students into small groups.

2. The hunt begins. In small groups, taking turns with the GPSr, students help each other mark their progress through the caches, marking the "final" cache with a large X.

3. In the classroom, students can transform their maps into stylized treasure maps that any pirate would be proud to take home.

Assessment

▶ Students will demonstrate their knowledge of cardinal directions and the use of navigation technology by successfully completing their geocache hunt and creating an accurate treasure map.

National Educational Technology Standards for Students Addressed

NETS•S 1a, b, c; 2a, d; 3d; 4a, b, c; 5b; 6a

Collect Them All?

No doubt some students will want to find each and every cache you've hidden. By focusing student attention on making a person-alized treasure map, the obsession to collect them all should be blunted. This lesson is designed with large classes in mind (if only one sequence of caches is available, the fun of the hunt will be lost after the first group completes it). As well, with multiple caches each group will create a slightly different treasure map. These maps can be shared with the larger class, and you can use these maps to show students where all the caches were hidden, both on paper and in the real world. All mysteries are thus revealed.

Multi-Cache: Type and Clues

The type of caches you place (large and small; real and virtual) and the sorts of clues and prizes you use to lead students from one cache to the next depend on a wide variety of factors—student age, class size, school setting, holiday season, weather, and more. As well, use this activity to support and reinforce learning in other subject areas (picture puzzles, math puzzles, word puzzles, and even Wherigo cartridges).

Locations with historical significance are ideal for setting up multi-caches. The first geocache in the multi-cache series can contain information about the historical significance of the area along with coordinates for a second geocache at another location that was involved in the historical event. The second geocache can contain additional information about the historical event along with coordinates for a third geocache at another location. This pattern can be continued until students have visited several locations involved in the historical event. The Freedom Trail in

Boston, Massachusetts, and the missions of San Diego, California, are excellent locations for multi-caches.

A multi-cache can also be set up to review mathematical formulas and calculations. Students can be directed to the first geocache in the multi-cache series. In this geocache, students can find a sheet of mathematical review questions. After solving the review questions, students can select highlighted numbers from the answers to use as coordinates for the second geocache. If the students perform the formula correctly, they will arrive at the coordinates of the second geocache in the multi-cache. This pattern can be repeated to create a multi-cache. If students cannot locate a geocache, they can check their calculations to see if they are performing the formula correctly.

Hopefully these examples have started your creative juices flowing to create your own multi-caches.

Enlist Outside Help

With a lot of students running around the school grounds, having outside help with managing and guiding a large group of students is a must. As you plan this lesson, send a letter home with your students outlining this activity and requesting parental help on the day(s) of the hunt. You may just find a few willing, able, and active geocachers in this cadre. These parents might even have a GPSr or two that your class could borrow for the duration of the lesson. Invite parents to help out. Don't be surprised, however, if you find yourself reminding parents that this activity is for the students.

Younger Students

Younger students will have trouble making the abstract connection between a GPS unit and cardinal directions. A lot of pre-teaching should be done to prepare students to make this leap of logic. Consider working in small groups (one at a time) with an adult facilitator throughout this lesson.

Making a Treasure Map

The online world is filled with some great how-to advice for making antique-looking pirate treasure maps. Two websites I particularly recommend:

How to Make a Pirate Treasure Map
www.momsminivan.com/article-pirates-map.html

Treasure Map—How to Make a Treasure Map
www.creativekidsathome.com/activities/activity_105.shtml

Classroom Geocache
Language Arts, Social Studies, Mathematics
Grade Levels 4–6 (ages 8–12)

Description

In groups, students will create a geocache and the story behind its existence.

Objectives

► Students will learn how to use a GPSr to mark a location and to average coordinates for waypoints.

► Students will demonstrate understanding of a work of literature or historical time period through creation of an appropriate geocache.

Materials

GPS receivers, pens or pencils and paper, compasses, various art supplies

Preparation

Prior to the lesson, educator will make the following selections:

► locations for placement of geocaches

► a story or time period that students will use to create the story of their group's classroom geocache

Procedures

► Students will create a story, based upon a literary unit or historical time period, that explains why their classroom geocache needs to be hidden.

- Students will create camouflage for their classroom geocache based upon the story or time period.

- Students will select SWAG for their geocache based upon the story or time period.

- Class will take the geocaches to the location selected by the teacher and select specific hiding places.

- Students will use their GPSr to mark the waypoint coordinates (location) of their geocache. Each member of the group then averages at least three sets of waypoints from the group to determine the actual coordinates of the geocache.

- Students will exchange waypoints with another group and find one another's geocaches.

Assessment

Students will demonstrate their knowledge of the time period or literature being studied by creating an appropriately camouflaged geocache with appropriate SWAG.

- Students will demonstrate their knowledge of coordinates and averages by successfully finding the geocache.

National Educational Technology Standards for Students Addressed

NETS•S 1a, b; 2a, b, d; 3a, b, d; 4a, b, c; 5b; 6a

Group Logistics

The class will probably travel together to the location where groups will hide their caches at the same time, creating a logistical challenge for the teacher. One way to keep a particular group from observing another group hiding their cache is to have North groups exchange waypoints with South groups, and East groups exchange waypoints with West groups.

Beginning Geocaching Lesson

Transplants
Natural Science
Grade Levels 6–8 (ages 10–14)

Description

Using GPS technology, students learn about the local plant populations and discover which plants are native to that area and which are invasive exotics—and where those invasive plants originated.

Objective

Students learn the difference between native and invasive plants.

Materials

GPS receivers, pens or pencils and paper, computers with Internet connectivity

Procedures

- ▶ Students are introduced to the concepts of geocaching—the activity, the types of caches, GPS technology, and so on.

- ▶ While students are learning about the concepts of global positioning (latitude/longitude, navigation, geography), they are introduced to the concept of native and invasive plants.

- ▶ Students learn about the native and invasive plants common to their area.

- ▶ Combining these two notions (GPS and plant types), students go on a geocaching expedition to locate and identify native and invasive plants. For younger students, educators can locate the plants they want their students to find and preload the appropriate coordinates into the GPS receivers.

►   Students create local maps of these locations and compare their maps to regional and state scientific maps that compare local and invasive plants.

►   As a follow-up exercise, students trace the origin of the invasive plants and compare their local ecology and climate to that of the foreign location.

Assessment

Students create a report that describes the local and invasive plants in their area and the distribution of these plants. Then students compare the climate and ecology of their local environment to those where the invasive plants originated.

National Educational Technology Standards for Students Addressed

NETS•S 1b, d; 2d; 3d; 4a, c; 5b; 6a

Plants on the Move

Follow-ups to this lesson can easily lead into other areas of the natural sciences and even transcend them. Students can investigate the hows and whys of invasive plant migrations, be they climate change, human activity, or other factors.

Beyond Geocaching

It is possible to lead students through this lesson without touching on geocaching at all. Education Kits that feature GPS technology to document invasive plant species are available online. The University of Wisconsin-Stout's biology department has created an invasive plant species education kit, and the U.S.

Department of Agriculture offers a similar kit on their website. These are large-scale projects in which data is taken, downloaded, and studied. This lesson can become a long-term project that, over long periods of time, can demonstrate the effectiveness (or lack thereof) particular treatments to get rid of invasive species.

Invasive Plant Species Education Kit
www.uwstout.edu/faculty/jamesk/Invasive_
Plant/Invasive_Plant.htm

Invasive Species: Manager's Tool Kit
www.invasivespeciesinfo.gov/toolkit/detweed.shtml

Intermediate Geocaching Lesson

Where in the World Has Our Travel Bug Traveled?

English Language Arts, History-Social Science

Grade Levels 3–5 (ages 7–11)

Description

Working as a group, students develop a biography and a destination objective for their class travel bug (TB). On Geocaching.com, students develop a profile for their travel bug and report its geocaching travels.

Objective

Students will learn about different cultures through the travels of the classroom travel bug and its hitchhiker.

Materials

Travel Bug—shop.groundspeak.com

Flat Stanley—www.flatstanley.com

Luggage tag

Procedures

► Students are introduced to the concept of geocaching in general, and travel bugs specifically.

► Once students are familiar with geocaching, students will acquire a travel bug for the entire class. This travel bug and its hitchhiker can serve as the class mascot throughout the school year.

- Once a class has settled on a travel bug and hitchhiker, students log on to Geocaching.com to activate their travel bug, develop the travel bug's biography, and upload a photo of the travel bug in the profile section of the travel bug's page.

- Students set a destination goal (e.g., TB will have its picture taken on the Great Wall of China) and/or travel objectives. (At each TB stop, geocachers will be asked to provide a weather report and one important fact about their city or area in their log entry.)

- Students summarize the itinerary for the travel bug on the luggage tag and attach it to the travel bug for the journey.

- As the travel bug is found and moved by geocachers, students supplement the travel log with information about each stop. Students supplement information provided by geocachers with information from research.

Assessment

Small student groups give short presentations, incorporating three facts about each stop of the travel bug after each location log.

National Educational Technology Standards for Students Addressed

NETS•S 1b; 2c, d; 3d; 4a; 5b; 6a

Travel Log Over the Long Haul

Students should be encouraged to create many different ways to keep track of their travel bugs. Ideas include logging the distance between caches, logging the local weather versus the typical weather found at the cache, and interesting facts about each cache location. You can also keep a running list of the number of moves each travel bug has made, which travel bug has traveled the farthest, which is the closest, which has moved the most times, and so on. This process demonstrates long-term data collection in action—a true scientific process—and creates continuity for an entire year's worth of class study.

See the World

Not only will students want to see their travel bug reach the final destination, they will probably like to see the travel bug at the stops along the way. This can be arranged by including a request for photos of the travel bug on Geocaching.com. This will make the project similar to the Flat Stanley project (www.flatstanley.com). Another possibility is to make a single-use camera part of the travel bug. Once the camera is full, ask geocachers to mail it back to the class for developing and posting to Geocaching.com.

Who Is Flat Stanley?

Flat Stanley has been traveling the world since 1995. In essence, Flat Stanley is a penpal activity inspired by Jeff Brown's Flat Stanley children's books. As a class, students create a trackable item (a paper cutout figure called "Flat Stanley") that they send to select recipients. These recipients return Flat Stanley to its owners, oftentimes complete with pictures and other mementos of the visit.

For more information about travel bugs, and to see a class travel bug in action, please visit:

Travel Bug Gallery
www.geocaching.com/track/gallery.aspx

Travel Bug FAQ
www.geocaching.com/track/faq.aspx

Travel Bug Class Mascot
Tracking Number: TBF593
Whitnall Middle School, Greenfield, Wisconsin
www.geocaching.com/track/

Intermediate Geocaching Lesson

Real World RPG

Computer Programming, Language Arts

Grade Levels 9–12 (ages 13–18)

This lesson features Wherigo cartridges. These "cartridges" are actually software games that can be straightforward experiences designed merely to enhance a geocaching experience for users, or they can be incredibly complicated adventure puzzles. New cartridges are published all the time. Check Wherigo.com for the latest and greatest cartridges. My favorites include "The Arena" (an homage to the *Star Trek* episode "Arena") and "J2B2: Village Robot" (a puzzle-solving adventure that takes place in Seattle's Gasworks Park). For more information about Wherigo, please see the section "Wherigo: The Ultimate Virtual Multi-Cache" in Chapter 3.

Description

Drawing inspiration from their local community and pop culture, students will create a real-world role-playing game (RPG) in the form of a Wherigo cartridge—role-playing adventures played in the real world via a GPSr.

Objective

Students will develop computer programming skills and learn the art of game design (storytelling) and product promotion.

Materials

Computer with Internet connection, Wherigo Builder software (free), Wherigo-compatible GPSr, choose-your-own-adventure books, role-playing games (RPGs)

Procedures

- ▶ Students study the art of interactive storytelling. Choose-your-own-adventure books and RPGs serve as models.

- ▶ Students are introduced to Wherigo.com, where they will download the Wherigo Builder software and play select Wherigo cartridges on a computer via a game-play emulator.

- ▶ Using the Wherigo Building Tutorial and other online resources, students are shown how to build a basic cartridge, in addition to other skills.

- ▶ Drawing inspiration from a variety of sources, students outline an adventure suitable for a Wherigo cartridge, and use the Wherigo Builder to create a working cartridge.

- ▶ Once students complete their cartridges, they upload them to Wherigo.com for others to play. Students promote their cartridges on Wherigo.com.

Assessment

Students successfully build a complete Wherigo cartridge. Fellow students and other Wherigo users are able to successfully play the cartridge.

National Educational Technology Standards for Students Addressed

NETS•S 1a, b, c; 2a, b, d; 4a, b; 5b; 6a, c

Getting the FAQs

Wherigo.com has an extensive FAQ section that outlines exactly what Wherigo is, how to build and play a Wherigo cartridge, and more. Visit their website at www.wherigo.com/faq.aspx.

The Development Team

For some students, storytelling will be the most difficult part of this project; for others, it will be the actual programming; and for others, it will be promoting the work online. To help students overcome these difficulties, a Wherigo cartridge can be created via a development team concept (in which each member is responsible for a different aspect of the project). This team structure mimics the game development process in the real world.

Enhanced Geocaching Lesson

What Season Is It?
Natural Science
Grade Levels 6–8 (ages 10–14)

Description

Students will track weather changes during different seasons and at different locations.

Objective

Students learn the relationships between location, seasons, and weather.

Materials

Thermometer, single-use camera, materials for a medium-sized geocache, computers with Internet access

Procedures

▶ Students will create a list of data that they would like collected, and questions that they would like answered, each time the class geocache is found.

▶ Teacher will place a geocache, equipped with the student questions, a thermometer, and a single-use camera.

▶ Students will record and graph the data collected from the cache via posts on Geocaching.com and record the responses to the questions in a journal.

Assessment

Students will diagram and graph the similarities and differences among the seasons.

National Educational Technology Standards for Students Addressed

NETS•S 1d; 2a, d; 3a, b, d; 4a, b, c; 5b; 6a

Gather Data From Around the World

Teachers can help students study the seasons around the world by asking geocaching teachers from different hemispheres to create similar geocaches. These geocaches will provide additional data points for the students, and allow them to compare when seasons occur in different hemispheres.

Enhanced Geocaching Lesson

Creating Virtual Geocaches

History, Social Studies

Grade Levels 6–8 (ages 10–14)

Description

Students will review a historical event by creating paths for virtual geocaches and adding placemarks to an existing map.

Objective

Students will select a series of places associated with an important historical event and explain each location's role in the event.

Materials

Google Maps or Google Earth

Preparation

Prior to the lesson, educator will:

► Teach students how to use Google Maps or Google Earth, emphasizing the creation of placemarks and paths.

Procedures

► Students will select an important historical event and three to five places associated with that event.

► Students will create placemarks in Google Earth or Google Maps as virtual geocaches for the locations. The virtual geocaches will include text information, images, and even embedded videos that explain the locations' significance to the event.

▶ Students will relate these virtual geocaches to the historical event through a path using Google Earth or Google Maps.

▶ Students will share their path of virtual geocaches with the class.

Assessment

Students will generate a report that explains their reasoning for selecting their virtual geocaches.

National Educational Technology Standards for Students Addressed
NETS•S 1a, b; 2a, b; 4a, b; 5b; 6b

Google Lit Trips

This lesson is not limited to recreating historical events. The GoogleLitTrips website (www.googlelittrips.org) demonstrates how this lesson can be used to bring a geographical perspective to stories such as Robert McCloskey's *Make Way for Ducklings*.

Enhanced Geocaching Lesson

Geocaching Podcasts
English Language Arts, Science, Social Studies
Grade Levels 6–8 (ages 10–14)

Description

Students will create a podcast in response to prompts from a geocache.

Objective

Students learn how to accurately report on an event.

Materials

GPSr, mobile phones or digital voice recorders, computer with Internet connectivity, and Gabcast or Yodio

Procedures

▶ Teacher will either select or create a geocache for the class to find. Student teams will be provided with a series of questions that they need to answer upon finding the geocache.

▶ In preparation for finding the geocache, students will develop a script for recording their podcast, which will include answers to the geocaching questions.

▶ Upon discovering the geocache, student teams will use mobile phones or voice recorders to record their responses to the geocaching questions.

▶ Students will listen to the podcasts created by the class, and discuss the answers. Students will create comments with corrections or additional information in response to the podcasts.

Assessment

Students will be assessed on the accuracy and completeness of their recorded responses to the questions left in the geocache.

National Educational Technology Standards for Students Addressed

NETS•S 2b, d; 3b; 5b; 6a, b

Create a Podcast by Phone

There are a number of low-cost services that provide teachers with a toll-free phone number that students can use to record their podcast responses. Gabcast (www.gabcast.com) sells this service for $.10/minute, and Yodio (www.yodio.com) is free. Gabcast will host podcasts created by students for free. If you just need a service that creates digital audio versions of phone calls, apply for a free Google Voice account. Google Voice provides an MP3 version of phone calls that can be downloaded or embedded into websites.

This activity is ideally suited for classes on field trips. Often, parent volunteers can assist students by providing cell phones for the students to use to record their podcasts.

Get Permission

Note that many schools and districts restrict the use of personal electronic devices, so consult with your administration before proceeding. Likewise, parents should be notified that students will be using personal cell phones for class activities—parental permission and students' cell phone usage charges must be taken seriously.

Create a Podcast on the Computer

If students cannot use mobile phones or a classroom phone to create podcasts, there are several free audio recording software titles for both Windows and Mac computers. Audacity (http://audacity.sourceforge.net) is available for Windows, Mac, and Linux, and provides teachers and students with an easy way to create MP3 recordings. GarageBand, which comes with all Mac computers, also provides teachers and students with an easy way to create MP3 recordings.

Enhanced Geocaching Lesson

Podcache Audio Tours

History, Language Arts

Grade Levels 9–12 (ages 13–18)

Description

Students will create an informational podcache about their town or school.

Objective

Students create an audio tour to share selected information about their town or school.

Materials

GPSr, mobile phone, and materials to make a medium-sized geocache

Procedures

▶ Students select a significant place on campus or in town to place a geocache (following good geocaching etiquette).

▶ Students set the starting coordinates of their podcache audio tour.

▶ Students record an audio tour that: (a) explains how to get from the starting coordinates to the geocache; and (b) explains some of the history or points of interest along the way.

▶ Students place the geocache and distribute the podcache audio tour to the other students in the classroom.

Assessment

- ▶ The audio tour successfully leads listeners to the geocache.

- ▶ The tour and podcache successfully teach three interesting facts about the students' town or school.

National Educational Technology Standards for Students Addressed

NETS•S 1a, b; 2a, b, d; 4a, b; 5a, b; 6a

21st-Century Audio Tours

Museum aficionados have become accustomed to renting cassette players or audio wands to explain the exhibits as they wander through galleries. Adding audio recordings to geocaching provides teachers and students with the option to add indoor locations or provide background information during the geocaching adventure. For more information, and to listen to an example of a podcache, visit the PodCacher website and listen to *The Cannery Row Caboose.*

PodCacher: *The Cannery Row Caboose*
www.podcacher.com/?p=154

CHAPTER 6

Geocaching Professional Development

Introducing fellow education professionals to the sport of geocaching is a great way to foster teamwork. This is also a great way to demonstrate the classroom potential of geocaching to your colleagues. It's worth noting that the vast majority of educators who sign up for my workshops start out knowing little to nothing about geocaching and even less about handheld GPS receivers.

Geocaching in Education
Professional Development
Workshop Participants

Description

Working in small groups, participants embark on a multistage geocaching adventure. Each group verifies its progress on an accompanying worksheet and reports its experiences back to the larger group.

Objective

Participants will learn the basics of geocaching and get a guided, hands-on feel for hunting for a variety of geocaches.

Materials

GPS receivers, worksheet, pens or pencils, and camera-ready cell phones

Preparation

- ▶ Workshop participants will attend a lecture that explains the basics of geocaching—what it is, how it is done, terminology, and so on.

- ▶ Five geocaches will be prepared and hidden in advance of the workshop.

Procedures

- ▶ Participants are put into small groups and tasked with hunting for the five geocaches.

- ▶ Each group hunts for, and finds, the five geocaches described on the worksheet.

▶   After hunting for the five geocaches, the small groups return to the classroom and report their experiences to the entire group.

Assessment

▶   Participants will successfully complete the worksheet and articulate how closely their expectations were, or weren't, met.

▶   Participants are asked to consider how to incorporate geocaching into their own classrooms.

National Educational Technology Standards for Teachers Addressed

NETS•T 1b, d; 2a; 3a; 4c; 5a, c

Sample Worksheet

The worksheet on page 137 focuses the efforts of a small group of educators in California—and what is good for educators is also good for students. In the workshop's worksheet, note:

▶ The opening section reminds participants to note their starting point using GPS coordinates.

▶ Each numbered section gives the name of the cache and its GPS coordinates.

▶ The instructions for each cache tells participants exactly what to do to receive credit for "finding" it.

▶ All five caches require the use of a GPSr. Three of the five caches require additional technology (cell phone, podcasting, text messaging, camera, e-mailing) for participants to receive credit for a successful "find." Depending on the circumstances, all of the finds could easily require technology use, or none of them could require it.

This particular worksheet requires participants (in San José) to have at least one camera-enabled cell phone per group and be able (and willing) to make audio recordings and send text messages, e-mails, and photos. As you might expect, participants tend to accomplish these tech-centric activities with great enthusiasm.

A single-page worksheet like the one on page 137 can guide students of all ages through a multistage geocaching expedition.

Additional Resources

My website, A Burt's Eye View of the World, provides access to a podcast and slideshow of my geocaching workshop, among other geocaching treasures.

Geocaching Workshop Resources
http://burtlo.com/?page_id=70

Geocaching Activity Worksheet

My name: _____

My group's name: _____

Each member of the group should mark the waypoint in front of the convention center fountain. Once everyone has marked his or her coordinates, average the group's coordinates.

My coordinates: N _____

W _____

Group average: N _____

W _____

1. Find the official geocache, "Northern CA Solar System Model: Sol" (micro). (N 37 19.859 W 121 53.308). Each group member should sign the cache log.

2. Find the virtual cache at (N 37 19.910 W 121 53.402). Call 800–749-0632; use channel number 15693 and password 2468. Record a podcast (maximum one minute) that includes the following information:

   Group name: _____

   Sculpture name: _____

   One fact about the artist: _____

3. Find the virtual cache at (N 37 19.999 W 121 53.390). Send a text message to 41411 answering the question, "When can you ice skate in San José?"

4. Find the official virtual cache Pony Loom at (N 37 19.694 W 121 53.590). Use a camera phone to take your group's picture with your GPS receivers. E-mail the picture to the address indicated.

5. Find the official geocache High Water (micro) at (N 37 19.5000 W 121 53.429) or (N 37 19.528 W 121 53.426). Each group member should sign the cache log.

Resources

These sites provide educators with valuable and interesting ways to bring the sport of geocaching to students. Inspiration abounds online. Jump in!

Click2Map

www.click2map.com

A service that allows users to make maps online using Google Maps.

Click2Map: Coins and Bugs Map

www.click2map.com/maps/ECplus3/Map1

Click2Map in action—this map shows the location of a number of travel bugs and geocoins.

EarthCache Sites for Teachers

www.geosociety.org/Earthcache_Lessons

A free teacher's guide that helps introduce students to EarthCaching.

Flat Stanley (Travel Bug)

www.flatstanley.com

The home page of what is perhaps the ultimate travel bug.

GPS in Education Geocaching Forums

http://forums.groundspeak.com/GC/index.php?showforum=12

A very active forum where professional educators discuss all things geocaching.

"Geocachers on a New Learning Path"

www.bismarcktribune.com/articles/2005/10/23/news/life/104036.txt

A terrific news story about geocaching in the classroom.

Geocacher University

http://geocacher-u.com

Every activity needs a fan site … and every activity should be so lucky as to have a fan site such as this one.

Hi-Tech Hide & Seek

www.studio2b.org/lounge/gs_stuff/ip_tech.asp

Girl Scouts go high-tech when they go geocaching—this site shows how, complete with links to related sites.

New York Educational Geocaching Yahoo Group

http://groups.yahoo.com/group/nygps

Created in 2001, this group is open to all teachers and professional GPS users. The express mission of this group is "to create meaningful learning activities for students."

Podcacher Podcast

www.podcacher.com

Geocaching and Podcasting: two high-tech activities that were made to go together.

Shop Groundspeak

http://shop.groundspeak.com

The official online retail store of Geocaching.com. A world of official Travel Bugs and cache containers is one click away.

Glossary of GPS and Geocaching Terminology

Geocaching, like any other activity, has its own secret language. It's part of the fun. You will find a lot of strange terms used quite freely on Geocaching.com. Don't worry. Just follow me, your humble guide, to get in on the fun of this not-so-secret society. Remember, I will always be FTF!

BYOP—Bring Your Own Pencil/Pen
Some caches are too small to have room for a pen or pencil. This acronym lets players know they should bring along their own pen or pencil to sign the cache's logbook.

CITO—Cache In, Trash Out
A play on the old hiker adage, "trash in, trash out." More than an acronym, this is actually an environmental initiative in which geocachers pick up trash

located on the way to or from a cache. Read more about it on the
Official Global GPS Cache Hunt Site (www.geocaching.com/cito).

CNGT—Could Not Get To

If a player uses this term on Geocaching.com, it means the
geocacher found a cache but for some reason couldn't actually
retrieve it (to sign the logbook).

Discovered It

A common post on Geocaching.com that means a player found
(hence can log) a geocoin or travel bug in a cache but did not
move it to another cache.

DNF—Did Not Find

Geocachers who hunt for a cache but can't find it post this term
on Geocaching.com. This lets the person who hid the cache know
that he or she should check on the cache to make certain it hasn't
disappeared.

D/T—Difficulty/Terrain

Using the five-point scale, a person who places a cache rates the
difficulty of a given cache. With D standing for *difficulty*, and T
standing for *terrain*, Geocaching.com makes this rating obvious
for every cache.

FTF—First to Find

The most elusive—and arguably the most important—term on
Geocaching.com. Any geocacher can claim "First to Find" by
being the first to sign the logbook at the physical cache and log
the find on Geocaching.com.

FTL—First to Log

Players who are aced out on the rights to a first to find (FTF) can take solace in this posting. It means that a player who wasn't the first to find a cache was the first person to log the find on Geocaching.com. Players who geocache with smartphones and a cell signal, of course, can access Geocaching.com in the field and log the find in real time.

Geocoin

A general term used to describe a trackable token. Geocachers can pick up a geocoin from one cache and leave it in other. It's not uncommon for a geocoin to travel the world. Unique geocoins are often created by players and used as signature items.

Firsties

You would not believe the die-hard nature of some geocachers. They do more than receive instant e-mail notifications for the newest caches near to them—they take off on their lunch hour to find those caches. This isn't as crazy as it sounds. Seasoned geocachers know that a new cache might contain a token of real value—a gift card to Starbucks, for example—that the FTF player is welcome to claim. In this case, hard work and dedication have their just rewards. Including a valuable FTF prize is also a good way to entice players to hunt for your cache.

GPS—Global Positioning System

A system of satellites that, in conjunction with GPS receivers, help users determine their exact location on Earth. This system is used by all manner of industries and individuals, including geocachers.

GPSr—Global Positioning System Receiver

This is shorthand for a piece of equipment that can pick up (receive) GPS signals.

GZ—Ground Zero

X marks the spot … almost. Ground Zero is a term used to describe the place where your GPSr says you are zero feet/meters from a geocache. Lucky is the geocacher who can find a cache without doing anything more than standing on ground zero.

Hitchhiker

Typically attached to a travel bug, a hitchhiker is an item that moves from cache to cache. A hitchhiker might not be a coin or have an obviously trackable feature (like an attached travel bug), though it will come with some sort of traveling instructions and might even have a logbook. In fact, it might even be a logbook.

Logbook

This is the only item that needs to be in a geocache. A logbook can be as simple as a scrap of paper, or it can be something much more elaborate. Signing the logbook is how geocachers prove they actually found the cache. To get official credit for the find, however, geocachers must log the find on Geocaching.com.

 ## Logo—Leatherman variant

The Leatherman image is the unofficial logo of geocaching. It is a public domain image. (The official Geocaching.com logo, on the other hand, is copyrighted and is not in the public domain.)

LPC—Lamp Post Cache

This acronym refers to caches that are hidden at the base of municipal lamp posts, often under the skirting or in an access hole. No kidding. I shouldn't have to say this, but don't play with caches in or around any sort of electrical equipment. Even if the location looks safe, who's to say that the wiring inside hasn't been vandalized?

MIA—Missing in Action

Yes, sometimes caches disappear. Sometimes they are found again. Sometimes not. For geocachers who are certain that a cache is not a DNF through no fault of their own, then MIA is a most appropriate description.

Muggle

This term, borrowed from the Harry Potter novels (and in those novels meaning *nonmagic folk*), describes a person who does not know about geocaching. Geocachers have to be aware of muggles, especially in urban settings. After all, if you saw a stranger gleefully digging around in your neighbor's flower pot with one hand, and a GPSr in the other, what would you do? Be discreet, both when hunting for a cache and when hiding one—you don't want muggles to throw away your precious cache out of ignorance, nor do you want them calling the police.

Muggled

If a cache has gone MIA, especially in an urban setting, a geocacher might speculate that it's been "muggled." In other words, this geocacher suspects someone unfamiliar with geocaching (who probably doesn't even know such a thing exists), somehow found that cache and disposed of it. Muggled caches happen.

Multi-Cache/Offset Cache

Used interchangeably, these terms describe a series of caches that contain clues or instructions that, in turn, lead players to the actual (final) cache.

Park and Grab/Cache and Dash

As the term implies, these are readily accessible caches that allow geocachers to quickly park their vehicles, walk a few steps, find the cache, and move on down the road.

Placemark

A Google Maps term that has become a synonym for *waypoint*.

POI—Point of Interest

New GPS devices use this term to stand in for *waypoint* or *placemark*.

PQ—Pocket Query

A feature of Geocaching.com, a *Pocket Query* is a custom search performed for caches. The completed search can be e-mailed to you on a daily or weekly basis, and users can download up to 500 caches at one time—a handy feature for PDA and smartphone users on the go, or for anyone with a GPSr that can download data from a computer. This feature is only available for premium account members of Geocaching.com.

Signature Item

This is a SWAG item created by a geocacher, who then leaves it in a cache he or she finds (or hides), to let others know who visited (or stashed) a cache. A signature item can be anything, though common items include geocoins, cards, craft items, pins, and similar trinkets (e.g., a geocacher named Spiderlady might leave behind a black plastic spider in the caches she visits).

SWAG—Stuff We All Get

In geocaching lingo, *SWAG* refers to the treasure found in a geocache. These treasures do not need to be elaborate. Students are generally quite pleased to find Happy Meal toys or trinkets acquired from exhibit hall tables at conferences. Geocachers generally follow the "take one, leave one" principle with SWAG.

TB—Travel Bug

A *Travel Bug* is a dog tag with a unique serial number stamped on it. Official Travel Bugs are available only through Geocaching.com. Players attach a TB to an item and place that item in a cache; often the TB has specific travel goals (e.g., taking as many train rides as possible). Other geocachers pick up the item, and away it goes. Players can track the progress of a TB on Geocaching.com via its unique serial number, and they can view a map displaying the TB's movement.

TFTC—Thanks for the Cache

A common sign-off comment posted by users on Geocaching.com. TFTC lets the person who hid the cache know you had a good time.

TFTH—Thanks for the Hunt/Hide

This is another common sign-off comment on Geocaching.com. It is used interchangeably with TFTC.

TNLN—Took Nothing, Left Nothing

Believe it or not, some geocachers have no interest in swapping

SWAG. Their game is finding caches. This term is usually found in the logbook of the cache itself.

TNLNSL—Took Nothing, Left Nothing, Signed Log

This term is often associated with geocachers who have upward of 1,500–2,000 finds—people who find geocaches just to find them, post their find on Geocaching.com to get their number count up, and move on.

Waymarking

This is an activity which involves virtual caches and is found at Waymarking.com.

Waypoint

A waypoint is simply the latitude–longitude coordinates where a geocache is located. All GPS receivers allow you to enter, store, and retrieve waypoints. Waypoints are essential to geocaching—without them, all caches would be MIA. The terms *placemark* and *POI* are synonyms for the term waypoint.

National Educational Technology Standards

National Educational Technology Standards for Students (NETS•S)

All K–12 students should be prepared to meet the following standards and performance indicators.

1. Creativity and Innovation

    Students demonstrate creative thinking, construct knowledge, and develop innovative products and processes using technology. Students:

    a. apply existing knowledge to generate new ideas, products, or processes

    b. create original works as a means of personal or group expression

    c. use models and simulations to explore complex systems and issues

    d. identify trends and forecast possibilities

2. **Communication and Collaboration**

   Students use digital media and environments to communicate and work collaboratively, including at a distance, to support individual learning and contribute to the learning of others. Students:

   a. interact, collaborate, and publish with peers, experts, or others employing a variety of digital environments and media

   b. communicate information and ideas effectively to multiple audiences using a variety of media and formats

   c. develop cultural understanding and global awareness by engaging with learners of other cultures

   d. contribute to project teams to produce original works or solve problems

3. **Research and Information Fluency**

   Students apply digital tools to gather, evaluate, and use information. Students:

   a. plan strategies to guide inquiry

   b. locate, organize, analyze, evaluate, synthesize, and ethically use information from a variety of sources and media

   c. evaluate and select information sources and digital tools based on the appropriateness to specific tasks

   d. process data and report results

4. **Critical Thinking, Problem Solving, and Decision Making**

   Students use critical-thinking skills to plan and conduct research, manage projects, solve problems, and make informed decisions using appropriate digital tools and resources. Students:

   a. identify and define authentic problems and significant questions for investigation

   b. plan and manage activities to develop a solution or complete a project

   c. collect and analyze data to identify solutions and make informed decisions

   d. use multiple processes and diverse perspectives to explore alternative solutions

5. **Digital Citizenship**

   Students understand human, cultural, and societal issues related to technology and practice legal and ethical behavior. Students:

   a. advocate and practice the safe, legal, and responsible use of information and technology

   b. exhibit a positive attitude toward using technology that supports collaboration, learning, and productivity

   c. demonstrate personal responsibility for lifelong learning

   d. exhibit leadership for digital citizenship

6. **Technology Operations and Concepts**

   Students demonstrate a sound understanding of technology concepts, systems, and operations. Students:

   a. understand and use technology systems

   b. select and use applications effectively and productively

   c. troubleshoot systems and applications

   d. transfer current knowledge to the learning of new technologies

© 2007 International Society for Technology in Education (ISTE), www.iste.org. All rights reserved.

National Educational Technology Standards for Teachers (NETS•T)

All classroom teachers should be prepared to meet the following standards and performance indicators.

1. **Facilitate and Inspire Student Learning and Creativity**

   Teachers use their knowledge of subject matter, teaching and learning, and technology to facilitate experiences that advance student learning, creativity, and innovation in both face-to-face and virtual environments. Teachers:

   a. promote, support, and model creative and innovative thinking and inventiveness

   b. engage students in exploring real-world issues and solving authentic problems using digital tools and resources

   c. promote student reflection using collaborative tools to reveal and clarify students' conceptual understanding and thinking, planning, and creative processes

   d. model collaborative knowledge construction by engaging in learning with students, colleagues, and others in face-to-face and virtual environments

2. **Design and Develop Digital-Age Learning Experiences and Assessments**

   Teachers design, develop, and evaluate authentic learning experiences and assessments incorporating contemporary tools and resources to maximize content learning in context and to develop the knowledge, skills, and attitudes identified in the NETS•S. Teachers:

a. design or adapt relevant learning experiences that incorporate digital tools and resources to promote student learning and creativity

b. develop technology-enriched learning environments that enable all students to pursue their individual curiosities and become active participants in setting their own educational goals, managing their own learning, and assessing their own progress

c. customize and personalize learning activities to address students' diverse learning styles, working strategies, and abilities using digital tools and resources

d. provide students with multiple and varied formative and summative assessments aligned with content and technology standards and use resulting data to inform learning and teaching

3. **Model Digital-Age Work and Learning**

Teachers exhibit knowledge, skills, and work processes representative of an innovative professional in a global and digital society. Teachers:

a. demonstrate fluency in technology systems and the transfer of current knowledge to new technologies and situations

b. collaborate with students, peers, parents, and community members using digital tools and resources to support student success and innovation

c. communicate relevant information and ideas effectively to students, parents, and peers using a variety of digital-age media and formats

d. model and facilitate effective use of current and emerging digital tools to locate, analyze, evaluate, and use information resources to support research and learning

4. **Promote and Model Digital Citizenship and Responsibility**

Teachers understand local and global societal issues and responsibilities in an evolving digital culture and exhibit legal and ethical behavior in their professional practices. Teachers:

a. advocate, model, and teach safe, legal, and ethical use of digital information and technology, including respect for copyright, intellectual property, and the appropriate documentation of sources

b. address the diverse needs of all learners by using learner-centered strategies and providing equitable access to appropriate digital tools and resources

c. promote and model digital etiquette and responsible social interactions related to the use of technology and information

    d. develop and model cultural understanding and global awareness by engaging with colleagues and students of other cultures using digital-age communication and collaboration tools

5. **Engage in Professional Growth and Leadership**

   Teachers continuously improve their professional practice, model lifelong learning, and exhibit leadership in their school and professional community by promoting and demonstrating the effective use of digital tools and resources. Teachers:

   a. participate in local and global learning communities to explore creative applications of technology to improve student learning

   b. exhibit leadership by demonstrating a vision of technology infusion, participating in shared decision making and community building, and developing the leadership and technology skills of others

   c. evaluate and reflect on current research and professional practice on a regular basis to make effective use of existing and emerging digital tools and resources in support of student learning

   d. contribute to the effectiveness, vitality, and self-renewal of the teaching profession and of their school and community

Index

multi-cache (offset cache), 22, 46,
59, 148. *See also* Pirate Treasure
Maps lesson; Wherigo cache

N

NAD27 (North American Datum
1927) coordinates, 21
NAD83 (North American Datum
1983) coordinates, 21
national parks, geocaching in,
60–61
naturalists, activities with, 17–22
NETS•S (National Educational
Technology Standards for
Students), 151–154
NETS•T (National Educational
Technology Standards for
Teachers), 155–158
New York Educational Geocaching
Yahoo Group, 141

O

Official Global GPS Cache Hunt
Site, 3
offset cache. *See* multi-cache
online resources. *See* websites
outdoor education site, activities
at, 17–22

P

Park and Grab, 148
parks, geocaching in, 60–61
PC interface for GPSr, 28–29
physical education, 101
Pirate Treasure Maps lesson,
107–111
placemark. *See* waypoint
planning and preparations, 34–40,
94–98. *See also* equipment
hiding your own geocaches,
4–5, 82–88

location of assigned geocache,
checking out in advance,
95–96
locations of existing geocaches,
finding, 2–3, 34–40
maps of geocache area,
studying in advance, 98,
102–103
notifying someone where you'll
be going, 95
roles for students, assigning,
97, 98
pocket PCs, obtaining geocache
information from, 70–71
Pocket Queries (PQs), 37, 148
Podcache Audio Tours lesson,
131–132
Podcacher Podcast website, 141
PodCacher: *The Cannery Row
Caboose* website, 132
PodCacher website, 104
podcasting, 104
Geocaching Podcasts lesson,
128–130
Podcache Audio Tours lesson,
131–132
Point of Interest (POI). *See*
waypoint
posting geocaches, 88–90
PQs (Pocket Queries), 37, 148
promotional items in geocache,
56–57
puzzle cache, 46, 58
puzzles as review activities, 20–22

R

Real World RPG lesson, 121–123
regular-sized geocache, 44
resources. *See* websites
RPG (role-playing game), 121–123